GRATITUDE

*The Key to Unlock the Door
of God's Provision for His Children*

Rev. Wisdom Dafeamekpor

ENDORSEMENTS

When elderly, godly men begin to write, it is imperative that wise people purpose in their heart to read and thus do themselves a great favor by gleaning from years of experience packaged in a book.

I have known Rev. Wisdom Dafeamekpor for a long time, and this book penned by him is a box of wisdom showing what God loves: thanksgiving.

Like Rev. Wisdom rightly said, it is almost ingrained in the nature of man not to be grateful; however, it is clearly stated in Scripture that being thankful to God is His will.

It is a fact that, many times, we are thankful to God only when things are going well for us. We dance and sing and laugh. That is very easy to do, as God knows.

However, there are times when we experience painful and even horrendous moments in our lives, and we sometimes wonder how on earth we are to be thankful in such moments. It's literally a sacrifice to do so.

God can do to the human soul works that no man can do, such as healing broken hearts; and that is something to be thankful for.

Rev. Wisdom Dafeamekpor has allowed the Holy Spirit to really guide his hand to wisely and intelligently present this often unpreached topic on thanksgiving.

I implore you, dear reader, to study this book and understand God's will concerning thanksgiving. You will find out that giving thanks actually releases miracles. You will find out the benefits of thanksgiving and much more.

The peace of God that surpasses human understanding will then keep your heart. God bless you.

– Rev. Steve Mensah, *Senior Pastor*
Charismatic Evangelistic Ministry
Accra, Ghana

SPECIAL THANKS TO the great man of God, Rev. Wisdom Dafeamekpor, for giving me this opportunity to write a few words about his new book *Gratitude: The Key to Unlock the Doors of God's Provision for His Children.*

I read the book and I tell you, it's a book you cannot put down once you start reading it. The book clearly explains the necessity of the most important dimension in Christian life, that is gratitude.

Rev. Wisdom Dafeamekpor dealt with the subject matter with utmost care, notably employing historical examples from the life of Israelites, which was awesome. Every page in the book is packed with Spirit-inspired teaching and admonition that edifies the reader. The writer poured out his heart and his personal experience into this piece work, and you will be certainly blessed by reading this book.

The eighth chapter, "Thanksgiving to God—His Will for Daily Contentment" should be read again and again. Thanksgiving is the key to total deliverance, total healing and total abundance.

The monthly planner with points of praise is very practical and very helpful to me.

Read the book and pass it on to someone who might be waiting for a breakthrough in his or her life.

God bless you.

– Pastor Samuel Polumuri
Senior Pastor, Christ Prayer Place,
Editor, Suvisesham monthly, India

REV. WISDOM DAFEAMEKPOR's anointed writing reveals the heart of God all through-out his book "Gratitude". God is looking for people whose hearts are so full of the Word of God that they express thankfulness for all that God has done for them. This new book teaches us how we can show thankfulness in all the things that God is doing for us through Christ Jesus.

Each chapter shows us how to locate ourselves and to operate and express from our heart true gratitude toward our Heavenly Father in our daily lives.

Hebrews 4:12 says: For the word of God is quick, powerful, and sharper than any two-edged sword, piercing to the dividing asunder of soul and spirit, and of the joints and morrow, and is a discerner of the thoughts and intents of the heart:

The Scriptures on gratitude used in this book go straight into the hearts of the readers and produce the result that our Father God desires: the joyful expressing of our gratitude and thankfulness unto Him.

Hebrew 11:6 says: But without faith it is impossible to please Him: Expressing our gratitude toward God releases our faith and pleases Him.

Faith rejoices, gives thanks and is glad, while doubt despairs complains and is sad.

Reading this book on gratitude has moved my thankfulness to a higher level and I am sure everyone who reads it will have the same result.

– Carl Hibma, *Itinerant Minister*
Professor, Rhema Bible Training College
Tulsa, Oklahoma

*G*RATITUDE BY PASTOR Wisdom Dafeamekpor is a book that will enlighten you about the essence of being grateful. Gratitude brings wholeness, which is evident in the life of the one leper that came back to say thank you to Jesus in Luke 17:11-19. Even though the nine were healed, they were not made whole; but because the one decided to come back and say thank you to the Master, he was made whole. The healing of your body may have come, but there's more God wants to do in your life; however, it will take gratitude to unlock those blessings. This book will help you understand what gratitude to God is and the need to be grateful.

– Joe Mettle, *President*
Joe Mettle Ministries

THUS, "THE GREAT teacher is the one who turns your ears into eyes so that you can see the truth." This book on gratitude by Rev. Wisdom Dafeamekpor is an envoy that carries the secrets of life and a legacy to all of the human race. If some nations, churches, families, and organizations had applied the principles of this book, they would have avoided failures in leadership and in personal life.

Gratitude is therefore a must-read for all who desire to sustain and increase their level of prosperity in life. It is the key to enter new dimensions of God's blessings.

– Rt. Rev. Isaac Clive Mould
Action Chapel Church
Accra, Ghana

ACKNOWLEDGMENTS

I TAKE THIS OPPORTUNITY to express my gratitude to all those who have been a great blessing to me while serving in the ministry of our Lord Jesus Christ. Some have been a blessing to me spiritually and some have blessed me with material gifts and their love expressed in several ways. They have inspired me to think and consider the subject of this book—*Gratitude.* I acknowledge their great impact on my life.

For the production of this book, I owe a deep gratitude to the Grace Chapel Family in Accra, Ghana, especially those who have been on my neck to get this message in a book form, after listening to the series on the subject from the pulpit.

Lastly, God bless Angie Zachary for the immense work she has done in editing and proofreading this material!

TABLE OF CONTENTS

FOREWORD

GRATITUDE—IT IS the word and act that stirs both the heart of the Divine and humanity to step out into more acts of benevolence. Interestingly its absence could raise thoughts of disquiet and even move people from lofts of kindness to tree perches of apathy.

Life offers kindness, either solicited or not, in the midst of much cruelty and harshness. When windfalls of kindness blow our way, especially when undeserved, we are all faced with choices that must find expression either in words or actions. The Divine looks forward to gratitude, and humanity expects it. In the absence of gratitude, humanity develops a firm resolve not to repeat acts of kindness, while raised eyebrows of heaven ring out a complaint. The powers in the dark world of the Satanic kingdom would fiendishly exact their toll without mercy when it is invited to sit at the table of ingratitude. Many a long haul of intended goodness is short-lived and blessings curtailed when ingratitude is served either on the platter of ignorance or within teacups of carelessness.

We live in a world faced with eroding structures of good, a world where demands are more frequent than thanks, and expectations sometimes walk in the unreasonable and people often wrap themselves within the folds of incorrect entitlement. We live in a world where we take the many blessings that come our way as deserved and more often than not take benefactors for granted! Relationships are now mechanized with give and take to the point that the oil of gratitude that lubricates sweet fellowship and ensures longevity of kindness seems to be in short supply in our everyday language. If there's a need for us all to be reminded of the benefits of gratitude and the dire consequences of ingratitude, it is now.

So here comes Rev. Wisdom Dafeamekpor, a man whose teaching gift helped many people across the churches. Interestingly, there's more demand for this voice to be heard. A sermon might offer sound doctrine but might still leave its hearers without windows of application as witnessed in Acts of the Apostles when men asked Peter, "What shall we do?" In this book, Rev. Dafeamekpor once more proves his mettle and gives full vent to the grace upon his life and ministry as he weaves a tapestry calling out for gratitude. From the pages of the old to those of the new, he leaves no stone unturned as he brings us all to the place of active choices—the choice to be grateful or not. And more than choices, he places a quiet, unobtrusive demand upon us all to find ways to express our gratitude to God and men. The Body of Christ stands to gain so much from this great salvo of truth flowing from a man I greatly admire, a stickler for truth, and one who possesses a rare character of godliness. This book might suit corporate corridors too and the principles contained stand to benefit all. Gratitude must always be both thought and actions here on earth. Amazingly, if God borrows a boat to reach out to humanity, He does fill that boat with a great draught of fish. My sincere desire is for all to have this book, read it and practice the principles contained therein.

I recommend it to all with joy. Thank you, Rev. Wisdom Dafeamekpor, for this work. We are grateful.

– Rev. Ebenezer Markwei, *General Overseer*

Living Streams Ministries International

Accra, Ghana

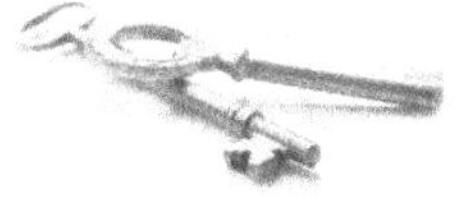

CHAPTER ONE

ONLY ONE OUT OF TEN

TEN LEPERS APPROACHED Jesus and requested His help for their miserable condition. At His command, they began the trip to the priest's house by faith; without seeing any healing with their eyes, they started their journey to get certification of their healing. They believed that somehow the Lord Jesus would do something special or unique for them. On the way to their destination, they suddenly saw they had unblemished skin as well as healed limbs and wounds. This was exactly what they had asked the Lord Jesus to do for them, and it would make a huge impact on their lives from that point on. They would be able to return to society and live normal lives once again. Their world had just changed drastically; they had just moved from one world into another altogether. How would they handle their joy and excitement?

Many delightful emotions swept over them—joy at the healing, wonder at the mode of operation of the Lord Jesus Christ, excitement at the prospect of living normal lives again, gladness for receiving a divine miracle, and anticipation about giving their testimony of healing to their loved ones.

But one additional emotion swept over one of those ten lepers who had been cured by the words of Jesus Christ. This emotion made him want to return and express gratitude to the one who had healed him. Such an emotion can be expressed only to the source of the blessing and can be understood only by the recipient of that blessing. This one out of ten stopped in his tracks to consider his priorities—where should he go first? The law was that the priest must certify the healing of a leper before the leper could rejoin society. Running to that destination would guarantee his immediate re-assimilation into society. But what about the Lord Jesus Christ, the source of his healing? Could he just walk away from Him without a word?

He felt he must go back; he felt compelled to express to Jesus his gratitude and appreciation in order to be satisfied within himself first. He felt the priest's certification—with all its benefits—could come after. To this one leper, having that attitude of gratitude and expressing it right away must be his first priority!

But why did only one out of ten feel this way? What was happening in the hearts and minds of the other nine? They had all been in the same difficult situation—plagued with the terrible disease of leprosy; they had all just experienced the healing which was about to transform their world. But only one had this attitude of gratitude.

MEMBERS OF THE "BLESS-ME" CLUB
IN THE BODY OF CHRIST

Since the ten lepers were traveling together, it's easy to imagine that the grateful one who returned most probably shared with the rest of the lepers how he felt about the need for them all to go back to express gratitude to their Healer. He very likely did not return without telling the others where he was headed. He probably even urged them, "Let us go back and thank the Master, Jesus, before showing ourselves to the priests." But the nine lepers were racing to their next level of blessing—their return to their families and society.

Today, in the body of Christ, many Christians move from one place to another (and from one church to another) seeking blessings each time. They appear to belong to the "you-must-bless-me club," whose members have little time to appreciate and express gratitude for how they have already been blessed. We can all learn from this one leper whose heart was bursting with gratitude. Put expressing your gratitude to the Lord Jesus on your priority list for each day. God is rich in mercy towards us. He lavishes His mercies on us daily. He is constant and consistent in showing us His mercies. Don't be like the majority in the world who take those mercies for granted.

The prophet recounted that His mercies toward us are renewed daily. *"Through the Lord's mercies we are not consumed, because His compassions fail not. They are new every morning"* (Lamentations 3:22-23a). Nevertheless, we should not take for granted His faithfulness in showing us these mercies daily. If we can recognize and appreciate them, we may be led to develop a heart of gratitude and be among the one out of ten who will return to the Lord to express gratitude daily.

On which side of the divide are you? The proportion (nine ungrateful healed lepers compared to one grateful healed leper) is too weighted in the direction of "take your blessing now and reach out for the next one right away." We need to examine this story further to see how we, too, can be that one out of ten with an attitude of gratitude.

"Silent gratitude isn't very much use to anyone who has done a lot for you."
– G. B. Stern

Chapter Two

Where Are the Nine?

"**S**O, JESUS ANSWERED *and said, 'Were there not ten cleansed? But where are the nine? Were there not any found who returned to give glory to God except this foreigner?' "* (Luke 17:17–18)

Upon seeing one grateful leper return to express his gratitude, the Lord Jesus asked him where the remaining healed lepers were and why they had not returned to express their gratitude also. His question implied that He was expecting all ten to show up. Let's look a little further into the events that led up to this question from our Lord.

Leprosy is a disease that attacks the body, leaving sores, missing fingers and toes, damaged limbs and a loss of sensation in the nerve endings which leads to more damage to more body parts. The affected flesh gives off a horrible stench. In some cases, the disease can take thirty years to run its full course. Worse than the physical pain that a leper feels is the emotional pain of having to be removed or banished from their community and family.

At the time when these lepers encountered Jesus, the law demanded that lepers roam together, shouting to warn others that they were approaching as they begged for food. They were complete outcasts from society. Even in Luke 17:11–19 when the ten lepers encountered the Lord Jesus, they had to stand "afar off" from where He was and shout out to Him, "Jesus, Master, have mercy on us!" When we consider the state of these lepers—the depth of suffering and humiliation they had to endure from the devastating and even deadly disease—and note what they had been delivered from, it is easy to imagine the relief they felt when they realized they had been healed. But what about gratitude?

We see in Luke 17 that it was the Lord Jesus Himself who directed the ten lepers to go and show themselves to the priests for certification for their healing. They were obviously eager to comply with Jesus' directive, which would restore them to society as well as to their families and loved ones. Their mission was very important to them—in fact, it was their top priority. It stands to reason that, upon noticing their healing, they would have been even more eager to reach their destination.

However, the one grateful leper experienced something more profound than the joy he felt at being healed. What he felt was even more pressing than the priority of certification by the priest. It motivated him to delay the requirements of the law as he sought to express the deep thankfulness in his soul that acknowledged help from an all-powerful and higher source. What this one leper experienced was a spontaneous outpouring of the gratitude he felt deep down in his heart. Everyone is capable of having faith for healing and even of receiving healing, but not everyone feels gratitude for what is received. And, not all who have grateful hearts are willing to express that gratitude.

Today, we know that Jesus' words carried life. He said in John 6:63b, *"The words that I speak to you are spirit, and they are life."* So when Jesus said to them, *"Go show yourselves to the priests,"* His words carried God's healing power to these ten lepers. Jesus' words also implied that they were healed, though that healing had not yet manifested to their physical eyes. As they believed His words as the merciful Savior and Master over all circumstances, including diseases, they took a step of faith by starting the journey to the priests. It was just a matter of time before their healing would manifest.

When their healing became visible, excitement broke out, and they were filled with joy. What were they to do then? The logical sequence of events would have been to quickly obtain their certification (which fulfilled the legal requirement) and then find Jesus to thank Him. However, being grateful and spontaneously expressing that gratitude is a work of the Spirit that is not under the legal requirement. Gratitude is a prompting of the Spirit of God that a person chooses to yield to, and the "one out of ten" felt this prompting deep in his heart. He realized that what had just happened to him was so life changing that he should express the gratitude in his heart to the Lord Jesus first—before anything else. He wanted to say "thank you" to Him immediately for changing his world—from a societal outcast to one being reintegrated into society. With the healing in his body, he could soon get back to his family and loved ones and hold his children on his lap again. He could work again and earn a living instead of being a beggar shouting at the top of his voice for food. The transformation he was about to experience was too great for him to ignore. In all likelihood, he had dreamed of being healed and restored to normal life one day, and that had become a reality at the word of the Lord Jesus Christ. He simply could not ignore this miracle of healing and the change in his circumstances. Expressing his gratitude became the number one item on his to do list. To him, it even superseded the requirement of the law that Jesus had commanded the lepers to fulfill.

So, this one grateful leper turned around and went back to the Lord Jesus where the Scripture tells us that he *"fell down on his face at His feet, giving Him thanks."* The account in the gospel of Luke says he glorified God with a loud voice. As a leper, though it was embarrassing, he had been required to beg people for food loudly from a distance. Now that he had been healed, he used that same loud voice to glorify God unashamedly.

The Lord Jesus was not surprised by the nine who did not return to give thanks and glorify God, though He did expect them to come back for several reasons. First of all, if one leper could see the need to show gratitude, then all ten should have been able to see that need. Jesus' question regarding their whereabouts was simply to point out how easy it is for many people to fail to have and express gratitude for God's acts of mercy and kindness. His question shows us that God expects us to have and be willing to **express gratitude first before anything else.** Since the fall, human nature is such that thanksgiving does not come to us naturally. The ratio of one out of ten says it all. Nine of the ten healed lepers considered their next blessing of being restored to society as more important than thanking God and the vessel He used to release healing into their lives.

Jesus expected all the lepers to return for a second reason. Their failure to express thankfulness becomes even more pronounced when we consider that it was the lepers who initially approached the Lord Jesus with their request: *"Jesus, Master, have mercy on us."* Their healing attested to the fact that the Master had shown them the mercy they had sought. It was only natural that they should have come back to thank Him for the mercy He had lavished on them. Their healing flowed from the mercy of God through the Lord Jesus Christ. Ephesians 2:4 says, *"But God, who is rich in mercy, because of His great love with which He loved us."* How many of us today seek and then enjoy His mercies without having or expressing gratitude to Him? It is so easy to take God's mercies for granted and fail to develop a heart of gratitude towards Him when He responds to our requests.

A third reason all ten lepers should have returned to the Lord Jesus immediately when they realized they had been healed was because of the method of healing that Jesus used. The Lord Jesus simply spoke His words of life to them. *"Go, show yourselves to the priests."* He demanded them to take steps of faith by their obedience. And they did obey as they set off to go to the priests. Their faith was rewarded as their healing was manifested later. Their joy and excitement should have made them come back to report to the Lord Jesus that the healing had happened just as He had implied it would. Gratitude would have demanded they tell Jesus what had transpired in their lives. Disappearing after the healing without reporting to the Healer simply displayed their ingratitude. Going back to the Lord to rejoice with Him over what had happened would have been a normal response from those who appreciate acts of kindness and mercy shown to them.

The Lord Jesus Christ asked this question in Luke 17:17-18 not because He didn't know the answer, but to point out the ingratitude and the frightening statistic that **nine out of ten failed to prioritize expressing their gratitude.**

What about you? Would you be counted among the one out of ten that has a fountain of gratitude gushing from the depths of your heart because of His acts of mercy towards you? Or do you fall into the category of the nine who are rushing to fulfill the legal requirement and be ushered on to the next blessing?

> "There is no such thing as gratitude unexpressed. If it is unexpressed, it is plain, old-fashioned ingratitude."
> —Robert Brault

If you fall among the nine, let us work together through this book on the attitude of gratitude that the Lord expects from us. Though it may appear that ingratitude is ingrained in all of mankind, the Lord can transform us to make us a part of the one out of ten who make expressions of gratitude a priority.

In the following chapters, we will see how the inability to recognize and appreciate God's goodness, mercies and kindness towards the children of Israel deeply affected their hearts and their relationship with God who delivered them out of Egypt. We will also see how, even today, a failure to have the attitude of gratitude towards God and other fellow human beings can deeply affect the human heart and drive us towards becoming negative people with little hope and joy in this life.

INGRATITUDE IN THE WILDERNESS

THE BIBLE IS a mirror in which we can see ourselves (James 1:23-25). When it comes to gratitude, the account of the children of Israel after they experienced deliverance from slavery in Egypt and were on their way to the Promised Land is a great eye-opener. We can learn a great deal about how to avoid ingratitude by examining how the Israelites responded to God's miraculous provision throughout their deliverance from Egypt and journey to the Promised Land.

FIRST DISPLAY OF INGRATITUDE:
Escaping the Egyptian Army

Setting the Israelites free from the oppression of the Egyptians was a dramatic and open display of God's miraculous protection over Israel. After the Israelites left Egypt and began their journey to the Promised Land, the first crisis they experienced in the wilderness was pursuit by the Egyptian army. The same Pharaoh who had urged them to leave Egypt after all the Egyptians' firstborn died had changed his mind and

> "An ungrateful man is like a hog under a tree eating acorns, but never looking up to see where they come from."
> —Timothy Dexter

now wanted them as slaves once again, and he sent his entire army and all the chariots in Egypt—including 600 of his choicest chariots and all of his horsemen—to bring them back. It seems that the more miracles of the Lord they witnessed, the more hardened Pharaoh and his soldiers became.

Behind them, far across the plains, the Israelites could see the galloping horses pulling the chariots and soldiers toward them. In front of them, they saw only the Red Sea, and they had no means of crossing it. They were helpless, and the disaster of being rounded up and taken back into slavery in Egypt was staring them in the face. Their situation was worse than what we normally refer to today as being caught between the devil and the deep blue sea.

Faced with that crisis, the Israelites' immediate response was to chide Moses severely. *"Then they said to Moses, 'Because there were no graves in Egypt, have you taken us away to die in the wilderness? Why have you so dealt with us to bring us up out of Egypt? Is this not the word that we told you in Egypt, saying, "Let us alone that we may serve the Egyptians"? For it would have been better for us to serve the Egyptians than that we should die in the wilderness"'* (Exodus 14:11).

This statement was a complete repudiation of their freedom from 430 years of slavery in Egypt. When they left Egypt, surely they were grateful for their freedom. But if they could utter such words within a couple of days, then we must ask whether they were truly grateful in the first place for their release? Did the gratitude they sang about end when their song was finished?

Nevertheless, our gracious Lord delivered them gloriously from the menace of the advancing Egyptian soldiers. Moses, having heard from the Lord, assured them, saying, *"Do not be afraid. Stand still, and see the salvation of the Lord, which He will accomplish for you today. For the Egyptians whom you see today, you shall see again no more forever"* (Exodus 14:13–14).

First of all, the Angel of God and the pillar of cloud moved behind the Israelites and provided darkness to the Egyptian camp and light to the Israelites all night long to prevent the army from finding the children of Israel. Then Moses stretched out his hand towards the Red Sea, and it began to part under the force of a strong east wind throughout the night. By the following morning the Red Sea had been parted in two, the waters forming walls on both sides with dry ground in between them. The children of Israel crossed the Red Sea walking on dry ground. What an awesome miracle from the Way-Maker!

Their deliverance didn't end there, however. The Egyptian soldiers saw the Jews marching through the Red Sea. To someone not used to the miracles and supernatural ways of the Lord God, this should have been an awe-inspiring sight. But the soldiers of Egypt, with their proud hearts, braved the frightening sight and continued to pursue the children of Israel into this battleground of water orchestrated by the Lord.

Next, God also made the wheels of the Egyptian chariots fly off so they could not reach the children of Israel. And while the Egyptians struggled with their chariots, Moses stretched his rod towards the Red Sea again, and the walls of water closed over the Egyptian soldiers with their broken chariots and confused horses, and not one of them survived. *"Thus Israel saw the great work which the Lord had done in Egypt; so, the people feared the Lord, and believed the Lord and His servant Moses"* (Exodus 14:31). This final act of their mind-boggling deliverance and display of God's favor and protection was when the Israelites witnessed the chariots and elite soldiers of the Egyptian army drown in the very place where they had just walked.

Thus, the children of Israel experienced God's supernatural protection from the Egyptian army. They saw how the Lord fought for them as He overran the chariots of the Egyptians during the chase. They saw the Red Sea part in two, and they walked through the middle of the sea on dry ground. They saw the sea obeying the commands of Moses (as the Lord directed him) as he stretched out his hand and closed the waters over the enemy army, and they saw the soldiers drown where they had passed through safely.

Moses burst out with his prophetic song of praise to God; Miriam responded with the timbrel (like our modern tambourine), and all the women joined in spontaneously, dancing with gratitude to God for such a wonderful deliverance. Just as one would expect, the Israelites responded with spontaneous praise, dancing and joy as recorded in Exodus 15—a glorious song which probably is what is referred to in Revelation 15:3-4 as the song of Moses which will be sung in heaven one day. The song begins with the exaltation of the Lord by the children of Israel as they joyfully expressed to God their heartfelt gratitude for His deliverance, protection and favor. *"Then Moses and the children of Israel sang this song unto the Lord, and spoke, saying: 'I will sing to the Lord, For He has triumphed gloriously! The horse and its rider, He has thrown into the sea! The Lord is my strength and song, And He has become my salvation; he is my God, and I will praise Him; My father's God, and I will exalt Him'"* (Exodus 15:1–2).

SECOND DISPLAY OF INGRATITUDE:
The Waters of Marah

Three days after their victory dance at the Red Sea, the Israelites arrived at Marah where the water was bitter and not good for drinking. Based on their recent experiences of protection and deliverance and their obvious gratitude—expressed in joyful song and dancing—it seems the most obvious course of action would have been for them to simply wait on their God for His next move to deliver them. However, notice their reaction: they grumbled against Moses. Though they had been grateful only three days earlier, at the first sign of a tough situation, they turned to complaining: *"And the people complained against Moses, saying, 'What shall we drink?'"* (Exodus 15:24). As astounding as it seems, they were unable to endure this test, remaining appreciative of the Lord's past deliverances and waiting for the next one from Him. They allowed a challenging situation to remove the gratitude from their hearts and introduced the poison of complaining instead.

Once again, God mercifully intervened and miraculously transformed the bitter water into sweet. He revealed to Moses that His provision had been there all along. He directed Moses to cut down a nearby tree and put it in the bitter water to transform it immediately to drinkable water. After that, God led the Israelites to Elim where the wells of water brought forth fresh waters.

The Israelites' failure to trust God in this situation raises questions about the sincerity of their gratitude following the crossing of the Red Sea. Being grateful and showing gratitude should affects one's character and conduct. If the Israelites really had been grateful to God for His deliverance from Egypt—the miracles of the plagues, the display of God's power on their behalf, His protection over them by drowning the Egyptians in the Red Sea—they would have waited in faith and trusted that God would provide them with water; but that isn't what happened.

Having an attitude of gratitude in the midst of challenging situations creates a strength of character which enables us to overcome the temptation to forget the goodness and mercies we have enjoyed in the past. Remembering God's goodness, kindness and favor with gratitude helps us resist negative tendencies such as complaining, grumbling and murmuring when we find ourselves in difficult moments. However, when we readily forget past blessings, then the change that gratitude should produce in us will be absent. Their responses to hardship make us, the readers of the account of their journey, wonder whether they were ever genuinely grateful to God.

Gratitude is much more than a brief song of praise. Instead of being a five-minute song, gratitude is a continuous state of appreciation in the heart. A genuinely grateful heart remains and will affect conduct, character and perspective on the issues that confront us in life. As we examine how the children of Israel dealt with difficulties on their journey, may we realize how needful it is to have a grateful heart and how easily ingratitude will introduce the poison of bitterness into our relationship with God. God yearns for a loving relationship with us that is characterized by joy, peace and contentment. Without daily appreciation and gratitude for His goodness and mercies, when difficulties arise in our lives, the poison of ingratitude and bitterness mars our relationship with Him, as it did in the case of the Israelites.

Complaining (against Moses and the plans of the Lord) came to the children of Israel more easily than trusting in faith and going through the fire of waiting on Him. A complaining attitude simply exposes the real state of the heart. A heart filled with gratitude is less prone to complain.

THIRD DISPLAY OF INGRATITUDE:
The Wilderness of Sin

In Exodus 16, the Israelites traveled to the wilderness of Sin, between Elim and Sinai, in the second month after they left Egypt. At the wilderness of Sin, they needed food. Apparently, the supplies they brought from Egypt were exhausted. Having just had drinking water provided for them supernaturally, one would have expected them to wait on God to provide food.

> "Happiness comes a lot easier when you stop complaining about your problems and you start being grateful for all the problems you don't have."
> —Anonymous

In all likelihood, they had expressed gratitude when the waters of Marah were made sweet. It simply stood to reason that their gratitude for the miracle at Marah would have influenced the way they saw their God and reacted to problems. They should have known that whatever their situation was, their God would come through for them. He had repeatedly shown that he would protect them from their enemies and provide what they needed.

But no! Instead, they started grumbling again when they needed food. Their complaints were so frequent and fervent that one has to wonder once again whether they had ever really been grateful to God for their freedom from slavery, their protection from the pursuing Egyptian army and the transformation of the bitter waters. If they had been truly grateful in those instances, they would have waited on the Lord to see how He would supply their need for food. Instead, their complaint went like this: And the children of Israel said to them [Moses and Aaron], *"Oh, that we had died by the hand of the LORD in the land of Egypt, when we sat by the pots of meat and when we ate bread to the full! For you have brought us out into this wilderness to kill this whole assembly with hunger"* (Exodus 16:3).

In their complaint, they showed little regard for the awesome and unmerited freedom that God had given them from more than four hundred years of slavery in Egypt. To use their own words, they preferred to die in Egypt with food on their tables rather than have freedom but go without food for some time in the wilderness. This statement negated every word of gratitude they had expressed to God about obtaining their freedom. These words could not have come from truly grateful hearts, which would not suddenly, in the face of difficulties, make a 180-degree turn and express a desire for the opposite of what the Lord had just done for them…for which they had sung His praises. Did they really prefer to be in Egypt to risking the exodus from Egypt for their freedom? We should ask ourselves today whether we also look back and wish we had not taken some journeys simply because of difficulties along the way.

The Israelites continued to complain and even went so far as daring to attribute a negative motive to God for giving them their freedom from slavery in Egypt: *"For you have brought us out into this wilderness to kill this whole assembly with hunger."* Despite everything that Moses told them, as he was commanded by God, they simply concluded that God's intention was to kill them with hunger in the wilderness. The truth was that, during Moses' encounter with God, he was told that He would deliver them from Egypt and take them into Canaan. This deliverance of Israel from Egypt was a fulfillment of what God promised Abraham, his friend, and the Israelites knew it. In Exodus 3:8, God's words to Moses were: *"So I have come down to deliver them out of the hand of the Egyptians, and to bring them up from that land to a good and large land, to a land flowing with milk and honey, to the place of the Canaanites and the Hittites and the Amorites and the Perizzites and the Hivites and the Jebusites"* (Exodus 3:8).

Moses had faithfully been echoing God's promise to take them to Canaan. Instead of complaining, they should have been talking about when they would reach that Promised Land. But now, faced with the challenge of having to wait a while for food, they accused God of intending to kill them. They forgot about the Promised Land where they were headed. What could have stopped this wrong accusation against God was simply genuine, heartfelt, true gratitude for their deliverance from the Egyptian oppression. How they could have wished to be enslaved in Egypt under their former oppressors, even with food on the table, is unimaginable. However, this was possible for the children of Israel because gratitude was absent from their hearts.

God's goodness to His children was again on full display as He started providing them with a daily supply of fresh manna for the next forty years. As long as they were in the wilderness, every day except the Sabbath, the Lord caused manna to rain from heaven for them. *"Then the Lord said to Moses, 'Behold, I will rain bread from heaven for you. And the people shall go out and gather a certain quota every day, that I may test them, whether they will walk in My law or not'"* (Exodus 16:4).

God's faithfulness towards us can be seen in His unfailing provision for us. God showed His faithfulness in sustaining them with fresh manna for forty years till they stepped into Canaan, despite their ingratitude. In verse 35 we read, *"And the children of Israel ate manna forty years, until they came to an inhabited land; they ate manna until they came to the border of the land of Canaan."*

Think about it for a minute: all along, before they ever uttered their awful complaints, the supply of daily manna had been available for them in the stores of heaven. But if they had refrained from complaining and continued to express their gratitude for what the Lord had done for them, their sweet fellowship with the Lord would have continued uninterrupted. The Lord would have opened the doors of the manna-store in heaven to them before they had cause to ask.

When faced with hardships and difficulties, expressing gratitude for what we have already enjoyed from the Lord in the past ensures our continued fellowship with the Lord. Expressing gratitude in such moments will build our faith and show our reliance on Him. Furthermore, expressing gratitude to God for what He has already provided for us unlocks the doors in His storehouse, giving us access to even more of His bounty.

The children of Israel miserably failed at this point. As the Lord turned on His tap of supply of daily manna for them, one would have thought that they had surely learned their much-needed lessons on gratitude by this time. They should have seen by now that the Lord had their best interests at heart and had provision and supply for them—whenever they reached the next point of their need, they simply had to wait on Him, believing that He would supply it all.

May God grant us the grace to be grateful people and have gratitude as part of our heartbeat towards God! An attitude of gratitude in the face of challenges helps us to look beyond the temporary problems and empowers us to exercise faith for solutions from God.

> "Spending today complaining about yesterday won't make tomorrow any better."
> —Anonymous

Fourth Display of Ingratitude: *Rephidim*

On their journey from the wilderness of Sin, they camped in Rephidim. (Exodus 17:1–7) Again, there was no water available. Surely, fresh from the experience of the bitter waters of Marah being transformed into good drinking water and currently seeing the daily manna falling for them, they should have said to one another, "Our God will do it again." They should have been exhorting one another to hold on in anticipation of God moving on their behalf and providing them with water. This faith-confession should have been that He had done it before and would surely do it again.

Alas! This was not their perspective at all. Exodus 17:2–3 reads like this: "*Therefore the people contended with Moses, and said, 'Give us water, that we may drink.' So Moses said to them, 'Why do you contend with me? Why do you tempt the Lord?' And the people…complained against Moses, and said, 'Why is it you have brought us up out of Egypt, to kill us and our children and our livestock with thirst?*" (Exodus 17:2–3).

Some people find it much easier to complain rather than express faith in and gratitude to the One who has brought them through previous difficulties to their current position. This is because instead of developing the habit, attitude and culture of being grateful people, they see gratitude as something to be expressed verbally using the words *thank you*. But real gratitude begins in the heart. The Israelites resorting to constant complaining and grumbling against the Lord aptly demonstrates that gratitude should not be a momentary affair.

———

The heart, which is at the core of our being, must be in a state of thankfulness for gratitude to flow from it. This gratitude from the heart or the core of our being will help us not to forget our past blessings. It will help us not resort to complaints.

"The worst person to be around is someone who complains about everything and appreciates nothing."
– Anonymous

The persistent complaints of the Israelites against the background of God's goodness and faithfulness as portrayed in the Word of God seem like horrible conduct to us today. An impassioned reader is tempted to ask them one question: why? However, remember that the Bible testifies of itself as a mirror. When we look into a mirror, we see the image of ourselves—whether we are dressed well or not, whether we look neat or unkempt.

One day, as I was pondering the lack of gratitude to God on the part of the Israelites, it occurred to me to ask whether that was the way I also had been relating to the Lord. Had I also forgotten His goodness in the past and been complaining at every point of difficulty? Is the picture of Israel, habitually complaining against God and forgetting His past blessings, a reflection of what our hearts are like today? Is the mirror of God's Word telling us "Look at yourself"? If that is the case, we should think about the horror we feel at the conduct of the Israelites and apply that fervid disapproval concerning their ingratitude to ourselves. We should abandon our lifestyle of ingratitude and its consequences of complaining and grumbling about the things we desire but do not have.

We should intentionally put on the attitude of gratitude and wait for the next door of God's provisions to be opened to us.

Of course, the Israelites thought they were complaining to Moses and Aaron. But Moses and Aaron were servants of God, acting under His direction. As they complained to Moses and Aaron, they were actually complaining to God. When complaints drop from our lips to other people in the midst of difficulties, we may also have to ask ourselves who we are really complaining to or against.

God's boundless goodness towards His children came to the fore again as He instructed Moses in Exodus 17:5-6, *"And the LORD said to Moses, 'Go on before the people, and take with you some of the elders of Israel. Also take in your hand your rod with which you struck the river, and go. Behold, I will stand before you there on the rock in Horeb; and you shall strike the rock, and water will come out of it, that the people may drink."* And Moses did so in the sight of the elders of Israel.

FIFTH DISPLAY OF INGRATITUDE:
At Kibroth Hattaavah

In Numbers 11:1–6, Moses and his entourage arrived in Kibroth Hattaavah. This time, it was the mixed multitude among them that yielded to an intense craving for meat, and the children of Israel wept as they cried out, *"Who will give us meat to eat?"* (Numbers 11:4)

At this point in their journey, the children of Israel were no longer complaining about hunger. In their journey out of Egypt, they had been given quail in the wilderness of Sin. *"And the LORD spoke to Mo-*

ses, saying, 'I have heard the complaints of the children of Israel. Speak to them, saying, At twilight you shall eat meat, and in the morning you shall be filled with bread. And you shall know that I am the LORD your God.' So it was that quails came up at evening and covered the camp, and in the morning the dew lay all around the camp" (Exodus 16:11–13). Thereafter, they had manna daily to satisfy their hunger. Their complaints now had to do with the type of food they were eating and what they craved or desired to eat. They wanted meat. If they were now desirous of meat, they should have remembered that the Lord had given them meat before and then manna daily. However, they once again easily resorted to complaining—because they had made it their habit.

The bondage of a complaining spirit, such as the children of Israel displayed, can easily be destroyed by learning to put on an attitude of gratitude and expressing gratitude for and remembrance of past mercies, provision and blessings. Even when we are in need, such remembrance should lead us to ask for today's provision with thankfulness for the past.

Here again, it appears that the Israelites had chosen to forget how the Lord had provided them with quail in the wilderness of Sin and then manna. Their complaints were always very fervent and persistent. They complained with such severity that it negated any gratitude they had expressed in the past. They expressed remembrance only of the supposedly good days and good things they had in Egypt. *"We remember the fish which we ate freely in Egypt, the cucumbers, the melons, the leeks, the onions, and the garlic; but now our whole being is dried up; there is nothing at all except this manna before our eyes!"* (Numbers 11:5-6)

This depth of complaint was indirectly a rejection of the freedom from slavery that God had given them. Lack of gratitude in our hearts leaves a vacuum which is filled easily by a complaining spirit. Complaints and grumblings, in effect, send out a message of rejection of the past mercies and blessings that we have enjoyed. Under the pressure of their immediate needs, the children of Israel expressed their preference for Egypt, where some of their needs were met, but in the midst of suffering and bondage. They did not value the freedom they had been given.

The Lord in His grace and goodness promised them the meat they wanted. *"Now a wind went out from the Lord, and it brought quail from the sea and left them fluttering near the camp, about a day's journey on this side and about a day's journey on the other side, all around the camp, and about two cubits above the surface of the ground. And the people stayed up all that day, all night, and all the next day, and gathered the quail (he who gathered least gathered ten homers); and they spread them out for themselves all around the camp"* (Numbers 11:31-32).

The lesson they should have learned by then was this: whatever they needed or wanted was already available in the supply house of God. If they had believed this, they would have also known that there was no need to despair, complain and grumble about their lack. They should have expressed confidence in their God, the provider. Even without their eyes beholding it, they should have been expressing confidence that their God would supply them with meat or whatever they needed, just as He had done in the past. Expressing gratitude, then, would have been their golden key to unlock the additional doors in God's warehouse.

Gratitude should also extend to what one is currently believing God will provide—even without seeing it. Being grateful to God for what we have not yet received shows confidence in the goodness of our God. The children of Israel appeared to be completely ungrateful to God for His past mercies and blessings. The sharp contrast between possessing a grateful heart towards God and displaying a plaintive attitude in moments of lack is so frightening to behold in the children of Israel. However, let us not forget that the Word is a mirror! As we look at the children of Israel against this backdrop of complaining and grumbling instead of gratitude, we must ask whether or not we are also looking at ourselves? How do we respond to God in our moments of lack? Do we stand in faith and recall His past goodness and mercies to us and begin to express our gratitude to Him? It is easy to be so conscious of what we lack—needs as well as wants—that we may also forget His past provision for us. We can avoid this only when we learn to become thankful to Him and deliberately express our gratitude as the one out of ten lepers did.

Expressing gratitude in moments of lack must be done intentionally. When we do not, we create a vacuum, just as the children of Israel did, that is filled with complaints that negate the joys of our past blessings. But who or what could have taught the children of Israel to be thankful and express gratitude to God when they experienced moments of need?

How can this attitude of gratitude be formed in us, too, so that we do not follow that evil, dangerous pattern in our own lives?

In their craving for meat, God showed not only His goodness, but also His anger against the complaining attitude and lack of gratitude in the hearts of His people. *"But while the meat was still between their teeth, before it was chewed, the wrath of the LORD was aroused against the people, and the Lord struck the people with a very great plague. So he called the name of that place Kibroth Hattaavah, because there they buried the people who had yielded to craving"* (Number 11:33-34).

Could this punishment administer the lesson they needed to learn? We will find out as we continue to review this next segment of their journey to the Promised Land, Canaan.

SIXTH DISPLAY OF INGRATITUDE:
The Wilderness of Zin

In Numbers 20:2–5, the children of Israel arrived in the wilderness of Zin where they once again faced the test of no water. *"Now there was no water for the congregation; so they gathered together against Moses and Aaron. And the people contended with Moses and spoke, saying: 'If only we had died when our brethren died before the LORD! Why have you brought up the assembly of the LORD into this wilderness, that we and our animals should die here? And why have you made us come up out of Egypt, to bring us to this evil place? It is not a place of grain or figs or vines or pomegranates; nor is there any water to drink.'"*

Amazingly, they continued to show ingratitude for their release from Egypt simply because of the difficulties they were facing at the time. They still had not learned the lesson of not complaining about current difficulties and remembering the past goodness of the Lord to them. Without the attitude of gratitude, their complaints once again expressly questioned the motive behind their deliverance from Egypt. They lamented that they had not seen the grains, figs, vines and pomegranates that Moses promised they would have in the Promised Land. This questioning implied that Moses had lied to them, which was in turn accusing God of lying also.

The Scripture says in Titus 1:2 that God cannot lie. When we question God regarding His promises and complain that we have not seen them, we repeat the conduct of ingratitude displayed by the Israelites. We must learn not to question God's integrity when the fulfillment of His promises to us appears to be delayed. Once He has promised, He will fulfil. He is faithful to His Word.

These complaints hit Moses so hard that he did the unthinkable before God. On this occasion, the Lord asked him to speak to the rock before him so that it would yield water. Moses, being provoked to anger by the incessant complaints of the children of Israel, struck the rock twice with his rod instead. Water came out for the children of Israel, but alas! Moses had transgressed before the Lord. What the Lord asked him to do specifically was speak to the rock, not strike it. Moses was so angry with the children of Israel that he first addressed them and said, *"Hear now, you rebels! Must we bring water for you out of this rock?"*(Numbers 20:10)

First, Moses should have spoken to the rock and not to the children of Israel. They were so rebellious that talking to them at that point was not going to yield any fruitful results. Secondly, it was by the Lord's supernatural hand that water was going to come forth from the rock. He is the Provider; He supplies all our needs. He was the One supplying and providing for the children of Israel miraculously—albeit through Moses. But Moses asked the children of Israel, *"Must we* [Moses and Aaron] *bring water for you out of this rock?"* The Lord had already told Moses to speak for the water to come out, but the provocation from the children of Israel through their incessant complaints to Moses and Aaron got under Moses' skin. In his frustration and emotional turmoil, he lifted the rod and struck the rock twice.

Paul revealed in 1 Corinthians 10:4 that the Rock following the children of Israel through the wilderness was Christ. When Moses chose to strike that rock for water due to his anger, he was inadvertently striking Jesus Christ, the Son of God. God was not pleased with that, and Moses received the severest punishment when God barred him from entering the Promised Land: *"Because you did not believe Me, to hallow Me in the eyes of the children of Israel, therefore you shall not bring this assembly into the land which I have given them"* (Numbers 20:12).

The ungrateful and complaining attitude of the children of Israel began to have consequences for others—most notably, their leaders. Almost everywhere in the world today, a complaining and grumbling congregation easily wears out its leaders and provokes them to anger. An angry leader, pastor or minister easily misses out on God's best, for himself as well as for the congregation. What happened to Moses was sad and grievous. In one moment of an angry emotional outburst, he took out his frustration on the rock by hitting it twice and missed out on the Promised Land.

Additionally, the children of Israel themselves were not allowed to enter the Promised Land due to their ingratitude, complaining and murmuring throughout their journey. In Numbers 14:22–24, we learn that the entire generation that left Egypt and started their journey through the wilderness was disqualified from entering due to their attitude of doubting God through complaining and unbelief. Only Joshua and Caleb, who had a different spirit, were exempted.

Gratitude and a positive attitude of faith set the stage for miracles and supernatural interventions to be performed by God in our lives and on our behalf. However, the opposite also holds true. A lifestyle of ingratitude and complaining leads to us missing out on God's best for our lives. But there is good news: we can cultivate the habit of being grateful and expressing that gratitude.

Why was it so hard for the children of Israel to do away with the poisonous habit of complaining and murmuring when they were in need? Why was it so difficult for them to develop a new habit of being grateful to God and expressing continual thanksgiving to Him, especially in their times of need? And today, why is it equally hard for some people to desist from constantly complaining and switch over to expressing thanksgiving to God for what He has already done for them? Is ingratitude naturally ingrained in us?

Perhaps for the children of Israel, one significant factor that contributed to their continuous complaints was that they had been in slavery in Egypt for over four hundred years. In Egypt, the rulers who followed Joseph oppressed them and gave them hard tasks to accomplish daily. They were beaten and kicked about unfairly by their Egyptians captors. They grew up complaining and murmuring at their masters and their lot in life. When God appeared to Moses to commission him to go and deliver them, He referred to their usual groanings. In Exodus 3:7, He told Moses, *"I have surely seen the oppression of My people who are in Egypt, and have heard their cry because of their taskmasters, for I know their sorrows."* They were an oppressed, sorrowful nation who had grown used to crying about their difficulties during their entire Egyptian captivity.

Though they were gloriously taken out of Egypt, it was not easy to take Egypt out of them. By means of great miracles, mighty displays of God's power and God's outstretched arm, they were delivered from Egypt. But Moses and Aaron could not transform them from a complaining congregation to an appreciative, thankful, worshipping and hopeful one that would exercise faith in times of their need. They were so used to complaining as slaves in Egypt that complaining and murmuring had become ingrained in them. In Egypt, they had little hope of escape and no hope of a better tomorrow in a better land elsewhere. They were gloomily eking out a life of survival from day to day. After the exodus, they had freedom from the physical prison of Egypt and were journeying to a Promised Land; but somehow, internally, they could not adapt to their new life and that great hope for the Promised Land. A transformation of their hearts and minds was required.

People without hope for tomorrow are usually locked up in the miseries of their past. They are unable to lift their eyes beyond misery and express trust and gratitude for what is ahead of them. The lesson for us is that we should learn to have hope for tomorrow. We must look back at where God has brought us from and conclude that since He has brought us this far, He will not leave us to struggle on our own in our difficulties. On that foundation, we can be filled with hope for our tomorrow. As we are told in Romans 15:13, *"Now may the God of hope fill you with all joy and peace in believing, **that you may abound in hope by the power of the Holy Spirit."***

Take a good look at yourself and examine your heart. Is it fixed on where God is taking you? Are you looking forward to a better tomorrow with hope or are you utterly consumed by the sorrows and oppression of your past to the extent that you are not able to appreciate what God is doing currently in your life? Are you able to look at God's provision for you in the past and feel grateful to Him even in the face of your current needs? If you are consumed with the sorrows and griefs of yesterday, even after you are delivered from your physical oppressors, it will be difficult to walk away from your internal attitudes of ingratitude, complaining and murmuring. It will be difficult for you to learn to appreciate God's blessings and express gratitude to Him when you face new difficulties in life. When you encounter a new need, those internal negative attitudes can overwhelm you.

Nevertheless, it is possible to make a transition internally and switch from a posture of ingratitude to expressing gratitude and thanksgiving to God, first in your heart and then with your lips. As we continue to look into the mirror of God's Word and see the examples of others, we find a pathway to developing a healthy habit of gratitude and thanksgiving when we come to moments of need.

As we have seen in the example of the Israelites, moments of need are merely times of testing. When we stand in gratitude, we see God as our Provider who has an endless supply of provision for us. Place your hope in God, and you will be able to exhibit an attitude of gratitude even in the face of challenging situations.

SEVENTH DISPLAY OF INGRATITUDE:
Discouraged on the Way

As they progressed on their circuitous journey, they became discouraged on the way. *"Then they journeyed from Mount Hor by the Way of the Red Sea, to go around the land of Edom; and the soul of the people became very discouraged on the way. And the people spoke against God and against Moses: 'Why have you brought us up out of Egypt to die in the wilderness? For there is no food and no water, and our soul loathes this worthless bread'"* (Numbers 21:4-5).

> "When we yield to discouragement, it usually is because we give too much thought to the past and to the future."
> —Therese of Lisieux

In response to this fresh round of complaints, the Lord removed

His protective hand from the camp of Israel. They were invaded by fiery serpents which bit many of them, and the people began to die. This was a hard lesson, but it finally brought the Israelites to their senses. They came to Moses and admitted that they had sinned; they admitted that, by their complaints, they had spoken against Moses and the Lord, and asked Moses to pray for the serpents to be taken away from their midst.

God forbid that we also suffer such punishments before we realize that ingratitude and complaining in difficult situations can attract divine judgment. It is better to develop a heart of gratitude for past blessings which should strengthen us to wait patiently for God's intervention in difficult times. A grateful heart recalls previous blessings and also expresses confidence and hope in God, the Source of our blessings, that He will provide for future needs. A grateful heart strengthens us to wait on Him without complaining in our difficult moments.

The Israelites failed to cultivate gratitude. Thus, they went from saying thank you one moment to complaining the next—until fiery serpents became their teachers. After their experience with the serpents, we see that they had finally learned their lesson, for when they came to Beer and needed water, they resorted to singing. *"Then Israel sang this song: 'Spring up, O well! All of you sing to it—The well the leaders sank, Dug by the nation's nobles, By the lawgiver, with their staves'"* (Numbers 21:17–18).

As we study these events in the lives of the children of Israel, may we choose to develop a heart of gratitude that is pleasing to the Lord—before He finds it necessary to punish us in order for us to learn its importance.

CHAPTER FOUR

CURING THE MALADY
OF INGRAINED INGRATITUDE

MOSES DID NOT leave the children of Israel alone with the ingratitude, complaining and murmuring they had adopted in Egypt ingrained in their hearts. If he had, God's rod of judgment and punishment would have been their only teacher on their journey. Though Moses knew that he was barred from entering the Promised Land, as a good leader, he wanted his people to succeed in reaching and inheriting the Promised Land. He thus began to tackle the ugly spectacle of carrying such wrong internal negative attitudes (ingratitude, complaining, murmuring) all the way into the Promised Land or into their future. He began to teach the Israelites how to cast off the effects of their life in Egypt and change their internal perspectives of their God, His deliverance, His daily provision, and His blessings in their lives.

> "It has been said that the sin of ingratitude is more serious than the sin of revenge. With revenge, we return evil for evil; but with ingratitude, we return evil for good."
> — W. Eugene Hansen

In their fortieth year in the wilderness, Moses assembled all the children of Israel together and began to explain the law to them—to remind them of how God had dealt with them thus far. He recounted to them a good summary of the history of their journey up to that point, as well as God's dealings with them. During all this time, their complaining attitude had not been lost on Moses. He subtly addressed that and explained to them God's perspective of the times He had brought them to a place where there was no water. *"And you shall remember that the* LORD *your God led you all the way these forty years in the wilderness, to humble you and test you, to know what was in your heart, whether you would keep His commandments or not. So He humbled you, allowed you to hunger, and fed you with manna which you did not know nor did your fathers know, that He might make you know that man shall not live by bread alone; but man lives by every word that proceeds from the mouth of the* LORD*"* (Deuteronomy 8:2–3).

Moses explained to the Israelites God's purpose for temporarily bringing them to a place of hunger and thirst. First, it was to test them, so they might know what was truly in their hearts. Secondly, those moments were to draw them closer to God and make them aware of their utter dependence on Him for their provision and supplies. They were to find strength and endurance in what God had earlier told them and look to God because of His faithfulness: *that He might make you know that man shall not live by bread alone; but man lives by every word that proceeds from the mouth of the Lord.* Thirdly, those moments were meant to humble them so that they could look to God and not assume it was their own goodness or intelligence that brought them through. These were some of God's purposes for allowing moments of temporary hunger and thirst on their journey.

Instead of depending on the Lord and looking up to Him in those times, what was truly in their hearts came to the fore—ingratitude for their deliverance, complaining, grumbling and doubting God's promises to take them to the Promised Land. In summary, the Israelites' ingrained ingratitude can be attributed to:

- Forgetfulness: they had a propensity to forget the goodness and kindness that the Lord had shown to them.

> "Gratitude is the memory of the heart."
> —Jean Baptiste Massieu

- Pride or not knowing how to humble themselves before God: They took God's provision for granted and were upset when the provisions did not arrive when they thought they should. Consequently, they didn't respond well to periods of going without said provisions.

- The slave mentality that Egypt pummeled into them: Complaining, grumbling and murmuring came to them more easily than appreciating the good aspects of their life. Living as slaves had taught them to complain and grumble about almost every treatment they received from their oppressors.

- Lack of appreciation for goodness displayed to them: No matter what God did for them, they were unable to maintain a spirit of appreciation for His past care.

Today, we may also face moments of lack and hunger or not have what we desire or need; we may face thirst or be in situations that leave us dissatisfied. Just like with the Israelites, these moments may be a test to reveal how we will respond. The Lord may allow tests to come our way—humbling moments that should drive us to seek the face of God for our comfort and survival. How we react or respond will reveal what is in our hearts. However, the account of the Israelites in the wilderness can teach us to intentionally determine to choose an attitude of gratitude towards God in such moments and refrain from voicing complaints and doubts concerning God's ability and willingness to be our Provider.

Moses was determined to change that ungrateful attitude in the Israelites. In Deuteronomy 8, as part of his discourse to them, he gave them good lessons on changing from ingratitude to gratitude and avoiding complaining and doubting God when they encountered moments of hunger, thirst and lack. These can be thought of as Moses' Lessons of Remembrance. Let us further explore these seven lessons that Moses gave the children of Israel to determine how they are meant to help cure the malady of ingratitude in us today.

LESSON ONE:
Remember God's leading and past deliverance.
(Deuteronomy 8:2)

Moses' first lesson was for the Israelites to always consider how far the Lord had brought them. He encouraged them to remember that

God had led them each step of the way, to humble and test them in order to discover what is in their hearts. *"And you shall remember that the LORD your God led you all the way these forty years in the wilderness, to humble and test you, to know what was in your heart, whether you would keep His commandments or not"* (Deuteronomy 8:2). Though it might have been through hills and valleys, good times and bad times, He alone, by His power, had brought them to where they were. Had the Lord not led them, they could have perished in the harsh conditions of the wilderness; they could have been devoured by the wild beasts of the wilderness. Through perils, dangers and difficulties the Lord did sustain them, and they were not destroyed. Therefore, if new difficulties came their way, they were to take courage and believe that the same God who had brought them that far in their journey would still see them through. Therefore, they were to avoid the doubting, complaining, and an ungrateful desire to return to Egypt.

It seems strange that the children of Israel chose to recall good memories of Egypt anytime they encountered difficulties—take the garlic, onions, cucumber, and leeks as an example. But in Exodus 2:7–8, God told Moses, *"I...have heard their cry because of their taskmasters...So I have come down to deliver them out of the hand of the Egyptians."* It seems the Israelites applied selective memory and deliberately chose not to remember the beatings, hard labor, and oppression that made them groan and cry to the Lord for deliverance. Consequently, they showed little gratitude to God. Their hearts were not resting and rooted in gratitude.

The same lesson applies to us today. When we look back on the difficulties that God has brought us through, we need not doubt His willingness to deliver us when we enter unforeseen or unexpected difficulties. Therefore, antidote number one to curing ingratitude and complaining is to always remember God's past leading and deliverances from difficult situations and dangers.

Lesson Two:
God has a divine purpose for our difficult moments.
(Deuteronomy 8:3)

Moses' second lesson of remembrance was regarding God's purpose for the difficult moments He brought them through. As you will recall, the children of Israel failed this test miserably on several occasions. Why were they grumbling? And why was this a sign of pride in the sight of God? They presumptuously assumed that since it was God who delivered them, God should make sure everything they needed was available before they arrived at each stopping point. They took God's provision for granted and expressed disappointment when the provision was not available on their timetable.

> "If we magnified blessings as much as we magnify disappointments, we would all be much happier."
> –John Wooden

Moses' lesson to the children of Israel was also meant to point out that delays were not God's denials. The delays simply afforded them the opportunity to show humility and dependence on God. These trials might appear severe in man's eyes, but God's purpose was this: *"...that He might make you know that man shall not live by bread alone; but man lives by every word that proceeds from the mouth of the Lord"* (Deuteronomy 8:3).

This is a tough lesson for many Christians to embrace. God brings us to times of testing and humbling to teach us to depend on Him. These are the times when we should fall on His mercies and deliberately seek His face. Do not question God's faithfulness or conclude that He has deserted you. Grumbling and complaining are a sign of pride in God's eyes. Keep your heart fixed on the Lord and let continuous thanksgiving, praise and worship flow out of your mouth. This demonstration of humility is what God wants to see during moments of difficulty.

When you come to a place where you are facing lack, hunger and thirst (or any other need), feed on God's Word. When what you are expecting does not arrive and your hands are empty, do not be angry and complain that the world is treating you unfairly. That is the moment for you to recall God's promises and what He has said in His Word concerning His provision. Your needs will be met. God is simply testing you for the moment to see how you will respond.

In Genesis 22:13–14, we read an account of Abraham passing just such a test: *"Then Abraham lifted his eyes and looked, and there behind him was a ram caught in a thicket by its horns. So Abraham went and took the ram, and offered it up for a burnt offering instead of his son. And Abraham called the name of the place, The-Lord-Will-Provide;*

*as it is said to this day, 'In the Mount of the L*ORD *it shall be provided'"* (Genesis 22:13–14).

Let it be ingrained in your heart that our God is a Provider. He will provide because He has already seen the need before you arrived. He is Jehovah-Jireh. There is no need to complain, grumble and murmur like the children of Israel. Even Isaac asked his father, Abraham, *"Look, the fire and the wood, but where is the lamb for a burnt offering?"* (Genesis 22:7). The experienced father, who had walked with God for many years and knew the dealings and ways of God, did not complain and grumble about what God was taking him through. He calmly responded, *"My son, God will provide for Himself the lamb for a burnt offering"* (Genesis 22:8). Let this be your faith-confession when you are perplexed about provision that is not in your hand. God will provide! Follow this up with your thanksgiving to Him, and the heavens will surely open over you.

LESSON THREE:
Remember God's past provisions.
(Deuteronomy 8:4)

The third lesson of remembrance that Moses gave was for the people to simply remember God's past provisions. One of the great miracles that the children of Israel enjoyed during their journey through the wilderness

> "If you don't like something, change it. If you can't change it, change your attitude. Don't complain."
>
> – Maya Angelou

had to do with their clothes and shoes. For forty years, their clothes did not wear out nor did they outgrow their shoes. Their clothes and shoes still fit even as their bodies changed; in fact, they lasted throughout the entire journey.

Did the Israelites notice this miracle? Obviously, they knew it happened; but did they truly recognize it as a miracle that was taking place every day? Or did they grow accustomed to it and take for granted that their shoes fit every day? Did they take for granted that their toes never got sore from tight shoes or that no holes appeared in the soles even after decades of wear?

It is easy to overlook the miracles that occur daily in our lives. They are easily taken for granted by all of humanity. Moses therefore reminded the Israelites that the miracle of their garments and shoes were big enough miracles to be remembered and celebrated. What daily miracles should you remember and acknowledge and thank God for today? As you rise from your bed each day, don't neglect to thank God for the miracles He bestows each day in your life.

LESSON FOUR:
Chastening from God is a proof of our relationship with Him.
(Deuteronomy 8:5)

According to Moses, the fourth lesson the children of Israel needed to remember about God that would cure the malady of ingratitude and lead them to be grateful to Him always was to have a different perspective on what they considered as unpleasant chastening from God.

He pointed out to them that a father chastens his son for the child's good. *"You should know in your heart that as a man chastens his son, so the* LORD *your God chastens you"* (Deuteronomy 8:5). Therefore, they needed to be thankful for the chastening, because it meant God was still treating them as His children.

The children of Israel were most certainly chastened by God during their journey through the wilderness. Chastening is not a pleasant experience for anyone. Those being chastened usually look at the experience as a sign of being out of favor with the one doing the chastening, and the Israelites were no exception. Because the children of Israel didn't have the right perspective on chastening, the more chastening they received, the more they complained about what they were going through.

> A complaining spirit prevents you from acknowledging those things for which you should be giving thanks.

Hebrews 5:5–6 teaches, *"My son, do not despise the chastening of the Lord, nor be discouraged when you are rebuked by Him; for whom the Lord loves He chastens, and scourges every son whom He receives."* Therefore, though it may be tough on the flesh when we come under the chastening of the Lord, we should be thankful. Chastening should not lead us to complain and thereby negate what God is doing in us. We should realize that it is coming from our Heavenly Father. Being left without chastening proves there is no father-son relationship with God, so be thankful for God's chastening as well as His blessing.

LESSON FIVE:

God promised to take them to a prosperous future.
(Deuteronomy 8:7–9)

Another reason Moses taught the Israelites to be thankful to God was to ensure that they were constantly mindful of God's promised destination. Moses sought to keep the vision of the Promised Land before them; he painted a vivid picture of what they should expect in the Promised Land and described the land as *"...a good land, a land of brooks of water, of fountains and springs, that flow out of valleys and hills; a land of wheat and barley, of vines and fig trees and pomegranates, a land of olive oil and honey; a land in which you will eat bread without scarcity, in which you will lack nothing; a land whose stones are iron and out of whose hills you can dig copper"* (Deuteronomy. 8:7–9).

> Constantly reminding ourselves that God is good— all the time — even when things are at their worst— is the best way to live and enjoy life to the full!

When we consider the promises regarding where God is taking us, we will have no choice but to be thankful. He is in our future, so we can trust that the future will be good for us. For that reason, we can be thankful instead of complaining and grumbling. We can have hope for a brighter tomorrow, even if the present appears to be a time of difficulty. Anyone who habitually thanks God for tomorrow will be unlocking God's storehouse of blessing in his life.

LESSON SIX:

When you have eaten and are full, remember to thank Him.
(Deuteronomy 8:10)

Moses continued his lessons on thanksgiving to the Israelites with this simple instruction: *"When you have eaten and are full, then you shall bless the Lord your God for the good land which He has given you"* (Deuteronomy 8:10). Most of us are accustomed to saying the blessing before meals. But, after meals, when we are full, we tend to be in a hurry to clear the table and move on to our next activity for the day. Few people wait to say a prayer of thanks to the Lord for the food they just ate. Moses' instruction is a good lesson for us too, but it actually went beyond a mere routine prayer after meals.

Moses told the Israelites that after eating they should remember to bless the Lord their God for the good land which He had given them. He wanted them to thank God for the land, the job, the ability to produce and all that God had given them that enabled them to produce the food on the table and all that they had. Moses was instructing the Israelites that their thanksgiving was not to be limited only to the food, but to every blessing from God—the good land which He had given them.

He told them that if they did not develop this habit of giving thanks to God for what they had, their hearts would be lifted in pride. Out of that pride, they would forget that God had been the source of their blessing. He was aptly describing the human heart to them. Their story in the wilderness journey was that when they came to difficult moments or places where they did not readily have what they needed, such as water, they forgot that God had been good to them in the past. They murmured against God and against Moses. They showed a great depth of ingratitude by their words and actions. Moses was instructing them to change from ingratitude to gratitude.

It would seem that Moses' lessons would have been limited to what they had to do in moments of difficulty, lack and deprivation. But no! Moses also drew their attention to another source of temptation to show ingratitude: *"...when you have eaten and are full, and have built beautiful houses and dwell in them; and when your herds and your flocks multiply, and your silver and your gold are multiplied, and all that you have is multiplied; when your heart is lifted up, and you forget the Lord your God...then you say in your heart, 'My power and the might of my hand have gained me this wealth'"* (Deuteronomy 8:12-14, 17).

According to Moses, when we are alive and full of every good thing that we have longed for, a subtle temptation comes to everybody to think pridefully that we have worked hard for what we have all by ourselves. We are tempted to take God out of the equation of our life experience. We are subtly tempted to forget God and subsequently attribute our wealth to ourselves.

King Uzziah, one of the kings of Israel, demonstrated coming into the good land and forgetting God. We find his story in 2 Chronicles 26. He became king of Judah at the tender age of sixteen and sought the face of God seriously and with his whole heart. He realized, like

Solomon did, that unless God gave him wisdom, he would not know how to rule a nation. He submitted to the instructions of the priest Zechariah who helped him and taught him well. As a result of his seeking God so wholeheartedly, God prospered him. He built cities and towers, dug wells, irrigation canals, and dams, and created numerous inventions in his time. He had successful agricultural programs going—large farms, livestock and great wealth. In addition, he was able to raise a well-equipped army to defend his nation. He was able to achieve all of this simply because God prospered him. His fame spread all over the region, and he was respected and known as a strong king.

Then, sadly, the Bible records that his heart was lifted up in him (with pride) to his destruction. One day, he decided that he did not need a priest to offer burnt offerings to God. He decided to offer the sacrifices himself, stepping into the priestly role of the nation. He went to the temple of the Lord to burn incense on the altar, and the priests tried to stop him. Eighty-one priests went after him to dissuade him. Under the old covenant, a strict separation of duties existed between kings and priests. Priests came from the tribe of Levi. You could be a priest and perform burnt offerings only if you were born of the tribe of Levi and, specifically, from the house of Aaron. That had been the law and practice for the Israelites for generations. In light of this, it seems impossible to imagine what came over King Uzziah.

When Azariah the priest tried to stop him, the king became furious with Azariah. Instantly, the Lord struck him and leprosy broke out on his forehead; he had to flee from the temple, and 2 Chronicles 26:21 states that King Uzziah was a leper until the day of his death.

How did this man go from being a nervous teenager who sought the face of God and was prospered by Him, to a famous, strong and wealthy king, to a forgotten leper living in isolation until he died? How did someone who was guided by a priest (Zechariah) into prosperity and wealth decide to ignore the counsel and advice of eighty-one priests who were pleading with him not to attempt making an offering on the altar? The fact was that, once he became wealthy, strong and famous, he had no regard for the priests. This happened because of the temptation that the "good land" brings. When the heart stops being grateful to the source of blessing and thanksgiving is absent from one's lips, pride, arrogance and disobedience move in quickly to fill the vacuum in the heart.

Hence, Moses' sixth lesson to the children of Israel was this: *when you come into a good land, and you have eaten and you are full, remember to bless the LORD your God.* The command *"bless the Lord"* means that you are to give thanks to God; adore Him and proclaim His goodness, saying what He means to you; proclaim that He is the source of your blessing and that without Him you could not have come into the "good land" you are in. The temptation to be lifted up in your heart with pride can be defeated by a lifestyle of gratitude and expressing that gratitude to God, the One who blesses you. Remembering and blessing the Lord with the fruit of your lips is a perfect antidote to the temptation of pride after coming into fullness and prosperity.

LESSON SEVEN:

Remember that your power to prosper and get wealth is a gift from God. (Deuteronomy 8:18)

The seventh remembrance that Moses wanted to give the children of Israel was that a) it was God who would give them power to get wealth, and b) there was a purpose for the wealth that He would give them. Moses submitted to the Israelites that if they would remember this always, they would be thankful for the wealth they acquired. Secondly, knowing and remembering the purpose for which God would give them wealth, they would not misuse it once they were blessed with it. They would not act like King Uzziah and become proud due to their prosperity.

When we remember that the power to get wealth comes from God, we will not give in to the type of complaining, murmuring and ingratitude with which the children of Israel usually greeted their difficulties. We will, instead, meet our moments of difficulty, lack, deprivation and need with an attitude of looking up to God and depending on Him for a turnaround. We will be in expectation of His intervention. When the children of Israel could not remember that God was their Provider, they could not thank Him during the difficult moments when they were without water or food. They forgot His past provisions and, on many occasions, even said they had it better in Egypt.

Today, we are on a journey with the same God who led the Israelites in the wilderness. Moses' instructions and lessons on remembering the Lord our God will help us move from ingratitude to gratitude. We, too, can apply these seven lessons when we have the option to remember the Lord in our lives. Doing so will help us express our gratitude as we bless the good name of the Lord.

In the next chapter, we will examine how David's remembrance of God's goodness made him thankful to God and enabled him to express His gratitude to God.

CHAPTER FIVE

THANKSGIVING IN THE LIFE OF KING DAVID

"*T*HEN *King David went in and sat before the* LORD, *and he said: 'Who am I, O Lord* GOD? *And what is my house, that You have brought me this far? And yet this was a small thing in Your sight, O Lord* GOD; *and You have also spoken of Your servant's house for a great while to come. Is this the manner of man, O Lord* GOD? *Now what more can David say to You? For You, Lord* GOD, *know Your servant. For Your word's sake, and according to Your own heart, You have done all these great things, to make Your servant know them'*" (2 Samuel 7:18–21).

David regularly gave thanks to God. In response to his desire to build a temple for the ark of the Lord, which represented God's presence among the children of Israel, God sent the prophet, Nathan, to him. Prophet Nathan informed David of God's promise to establish his house and kingdom forever. He gave him a covenant that God's mercy would not depart from David's seed and his kingdom would be forever.

David was overwhelmed by the promises given to him. He looked back on where he came from—the back side of a desert tending to his father's flock, not being recognized in his own father's house like his brothers. He recalled Saul's harassment and numerous attempts to kill him—and yet he ascended the throne as king of Israel. And now, God was promising him that his house and kingdom would be forever. He went into the tent where the ark of God was, sat in the presence of God and began a prayer of thanksgiving that revealed how he felt. Instead of just saying "thank You," he expressed heartfelt gratitude. He specifically recalled how the Lord had brought him to his present position. He applied the lesson Moses had given the children of Israel: always remember what God has done for you in the past. In order to be grateful to God, you need to look back at where you were and how God brought you to where you are currently.

Out of David's wonder for the goodness of God to him, he asked in his prayer of thanksgiving, *Who am I, O Lord God? And what is my house, that You have brought me this far?"* In other words, David recognized that he did not deserve what God had done for him; he recognized that God had blessed him because of who God is—good and gracious! He thanked God for bringing him to the throne; he did not assume the posture that God should have done it for him. The way the children of Israel complained in the wilderness when they came to a place of need implied that God should have foreseen their need and put what they needed in place before they arrived. This attitude and posture robbed them of looking up to God expectantly when in need and thanking Him with a grateful heart when He provided.

Without humility, we cannot thank God and express our gratitude to Him in an acceptable manner—we will lack the humility that will cause us to say, "I do not deserve this by my own efforts, but You have done it. It is because You are good and gracious to me." Thanksgiving flows from a heart of humility.

As David continued praying, he looked at what God had promised him. He expressed wonder at God's promises and continued to thank Him until words were no longer adequate. *"Now what more can David say to you?"*

Knowing David's history with music, it's likely that he broke out into songs of praise and worship. When the heart cannot find words before God, we often express ourselves in the next level of communication—singing. David is described as the sweet psalmist of Israel in 2 Samuel 23:1. In the presence of God, David would have burst out into a series of songs. It would have been a sweet time of communion and fellowship between David and God alone. The songs would not have been a performance on a stage to please a crowd of spectators but an expression from a heart of gratitude to the One who had brought him thus far in life.

May the Lord Himself bring each one reading this book to that place of expressing our gratitude to Him! May He change our hearts and give us hearts of gratitude rather than hearts that complain and murmur about what He has not yet provided!

Please allow me to share a personal illustration. Our church service was about to close when a friend who was one of the faithful longtime members asked me if he could give a testimony. I agreed, and he asked his whole family to stand with him. He began by saying how the Lord had blessed him since he came to the church. He said his business, a car dealership, had been thriving and, in appreciation, he had a small gift for me personally. He was holding a small packet in his hands. I wondered what it could be as I listened to his well-rehearsed speech of appreciation. I first thought it looked like a bar of neatly wrapped chocolate; then I was convinced it was a bottle of cologne.

He finished his speech, walked over to me and said, "In appreciation, we have this small packet for you." As I stretched out my hand to accept the gift, he added, "Outside is your brand-new car, and this is the key." That little packet contained the keys to a Land Cruiser. I slumped into my chair with shock, and the church broke into spontaneous dancing and jubilation. After the church service, I managed to find out how much the vehicle with all its add-ons would cost, and I was further overwhelmed.

In the Anlo-land in Ghana, where I grew up, our custom is to thank our benefactors at least twice—instantly when kindness is shown or a gift is given, and early in the morning one or two days later. Early in the morning the following day, I showed up at his house with my wife and three children to thank him. According to our custom, we were all seated, and they demanded to know our mission for showing up at their house so early in the morning. Of course, it was obvious, but according to the custom, I had to declare my mission formally before proceeding to express my thanks. Knowing how much such a valuable vehicle and all its add-ons cost my friend, I suddenly became overwhelmed once again and found myself speechless. I struggled but could not utter a sentence. Before I realized it, copious tears were flowing from my eyes. Too overwhelmed in my heart, I could not find words to even say thank you for such a valuable gift. No one knew that I had desired to have such a four-wheel drive for mission work and church planting projects out of the city. Yet it had been given to me without warning. I could only express my gratitude with tears.

What left me speechless was just a vehicle. It should not be surprising that the life-transforming experience God gave David—from being a forgotten shepherd boy to sitting on the throne as the king of Israel—left him without words to express his gratitude. He was so grateful to God, yet words were not adequate for him as he prayed. I believe he sang and worshipped out of gratitude, and that we should take a cue from David's example. When words become inadequate for you, what do you, personally, do? How do you express your gratitude to God? At a certain level, expressing gratitude can become emotional and heartfelt. If our gratitude brings tears, we should let them flow; and if our response is through music and singing, we should let it out joyfully.

I believe God has most certainly shown us all His goodness in our life journey so far; He has given grace and favor that would have transformed our lives positively. May God give us tender hearts that we will also become so overwhelmed with God's goodness and grace that we can express our gratitude at a level beyond words. God forbid that, like the nine lepers, we will be so hard-hearted that we just continue racing on in life toward our next blessing.

King David took the time to go into the tent of meeting and sit before the Lord just to express gratitude for transforming his life, and his expression went beyond words. In his prayer of thanksgiving, David affirmed the goodness and grace of God and pointed to other attributes as well. *"For Your word's sake, and according to Your own heart, You have done all these great things, to make Your servant know them"* (2 Samuel 7:21). That is what gratitude to God does in the thanksgiver. It causes him to see who God really is and appreciate His attributes. Seeing God as He is and getting to know His attributes helps us to remain grateful to Him.

Then David's passionate praise came springing forth like this: *"Therefore You are great, O Lord God. For there is none like You, nor is there any God besides You, according to all that we have heard with our ears...So let Your name be magnified forever, saying, 'The Lord of hosts is the God over Israel'"* (2 Samuel 7:22, 26a). One of the major differences between King David and King Saul, whom David succeeded, is David's expression of gratitude to God for his elevation to the throne. In no account of King Saul do we see him expressing such depth of gratitude to God. The difference in the results of David's grateful attitude and Saul's lack thereof is remarkable. To Saul, God said, *"But now your kingdom shall not continue. The Lord has sought for Himself a man after His own heart"* (1 Samuel 13:14a). To David, God said, *"And your house and your kingdom shall be established forever before you. Your throne shall be established forever"* (2 Samuel 7:16). On another occasion, Saul disobeyed God, and the prophet Samuel told him, *"The*

*Lord has torn the kingdom of Israel from you today, and has given it to a neighbor of yours **who is better than you**"* (1 Samuel 15:28). The attitude of gratitude makes one a better person and a candidate for more of God's blessings.

The attitude of gratitude softens the heart, making a person more apt to respond to God with obedience than someone who is not grateful. Perhaps Saul's stiff-necked disobedience to God would not have been so pronounced if he had developed and shown more gratitude to God like David did. Those who refuse to express gratitude for the blessings they enjoy eventually develop hardness in their hearts which later deprives them of God's continued blessings.

Someone Who Refused to Show Gratitude

We find the account of Nabal in 1 Samuel 25. This man refused to show gratitude to his benefactor, David, who protected his livestock at one time. David, while evading King Saul, dwelt in caves in the wilderness. During these times, he and his volunteer army of four hundred loyal followers came near Carmel, where Nabal lived. Nabal was rich in livestock, and his flocks of sheep and goats were targeted by armed robbers and bandits for a considerable time; as a result, he was losing money.

When David and his men came into Nabal's region, they protected Nabal's livestock from the marauders. David and his men did this for free and of their own volition because of their indignation over the actions of the robbers. As a result, Nabal's financial situation was improved.

One time, when David ran out of food, he sent ten of his servants to Nabal to ask for provisions. He told the men to remind Nabal of the free protection he had provided for his livestock. David anticipated that Nabal would be willing to reciprocate food in return, but Nabal harshly denied his request: *"Who is David, and who is the son of Jesse? There are many servants nowadays who break away each one from his master. Shall I then take my bread and my water and my meat that I have killed for my shearers, and give it to men when I do not know where they are from?"* (1 Samuel 25:10–11). One of Nabal's servants heard his response and ran to report to Nabal's wife, Abigail. He told her what David and his men had done for Nabal's herdsmen and described his master as a scoundrel for showing ingratitude. Abigail went to meet David with the food he had requested and pled with him not to retaliate against Nabal for his foolishness. *"Please, let not my lord regard this scoundrel Nabal. For as his name is, so is he: Nabal is his name, and folly is with him!"* (1 Samuel 25:25).

The name *Nabal* means "foolishness." Nabal foolishly failed to appreciate what David did for him and showed no gratitude at all. He took it all for granted because his heart had been hardened by his foolishness. A hardened heart is not moved easily, not by miracles nor even by goodness and kindness. Consequently, a hardened heart can repay evil for good, and those who repay evil for good usually bring curses upon themselves. 1 Samuel 25:38 sums it up: *"Then it happened, after about ten days, that the LORD struck Nabal, and he died."* That was the price Nabal paid for showing ingratitude to someone who had been kind to him. God takes gratitude more seriously than many of us think. If you have not developed the habit of being grateful yet, then it is time for you to start learning to thank your benefactors.

First, we should always be thankful to God in general for the life He has given us. Secondly, we should be grateful for the blessing of our redemption through His Son, Jesus Christ. We can never thank Him enough for that. If you have believed on the Lord Jesus Christ for salvation, and you compare your past life without Christ to your life in Christ Jesus, you will be so full of gratitude to God that you will sing songs of thanksgiving to Him daily. Thirdly, we cannot stop being grateful and thanking Him for where He is taking us, according to His Word of promise. The key factor to developing this heart of gratitude, as David has shown, is to remember where God has brought you from and where He is taking you to in the future.

The Price We Pay for Unthankfulness

Nabal paid an expensive price for refusing to show gratitude to David. His ingratitude came at the cost of his very life. Today, when we are not thankful to God for His ever-continuing mercies and goodness to us, we may find out that we are also in line to

"The unthankful heart discovers no mercies; but the thankful heart will find, in every hour, some heavenly blessings."
– Henry Ward Beecher

pay a price for our ingratitude. Paul revealed in his epistle to the Romans that there is a price to pay when we refuse to be grateful to God. *"For since the creation of the world His invisible attributes are clearly* *seen, being understood by the things that are made, even His eternal power and Godhead, so that they are without excuse, because, although they knew God, **they did not glorify Him as God, nor were thankful,** but became futile in their thoughts, and their foolish hearts were darkened. Professing to be wise, they became fools…Therefore God also gave them up to uncleanness, in the lusts of their hearts…For this reason God gave them up to vile passions. For even their women exchanged the natural use for what is against nature. Likewise also the men, leaving the natural use of the woman, burned in their lust for one another, men with men committing what is shameful, and receiving in themselves the penalty of their error which was due"* (Romans 1:20–27).

God considers people who neither glorify nor thank Him for His attributes and eternal power as being without excuse, for knowing God and His attributes should not be difficult to humanity. His power can be seen and known by everyone. His attributes are revealed in nature around us. *"Because what may be known of God is manifest in them* [the human race] *because God has shown it to them* [every one of us]*"* (Romans 1:19). So why do some people claim alternate theories of how the world came into existence instead of believing that God, our sovereign Lord, made the world? Those who claim that a sovereign God who made heaven and earth does not exist at all have to deliberately choose to ignore the evidence that God has revealed in the heart of every one of us. Long before Paul wrote his epistle to the Romans, David testified in Psalm 19 to the general revelation of God to the whole human race: *"The heavens declare the glory of God;*

and the firmament shows His handiwork. Day unto day utters speech, and night unto night reveals knowledge. There is no speech nor language where their voice is not heard. Their line has gone out through all the earth, And their words to the end of the world. In them He has set a tabernacle for the sun" (Psalm 19:1–4).

Therefore, the knowledge of God cannot be lost on anyone who simply looks around us at nature—we see the firmament, sun, night, moon, mountains, hills, valleys, rivers and many more evidences of the Maker of the universe. What then do we do with the knowledge of God which He has given us in our hearts? Since within our very being we know the truth of the existence of God, we must glorify Him and be thankful to Him for His attributes that we can plainly see at work in our lives. His existence and attributes should so overwhelm us that we should freely worship Him and express our gratitude to Him for being our God. It is He, God, who made us and sustains us and the universe day by day.

Paul, in his epistle to the Romans, submitted that those who deny the existence of God have deliberately suppressed the truth in un-righteousness. Once they deny the existence of God, they cannot and do not glorify Him and cannot express any gratitude to Him. Consequently, the wrath of God is revealed from heaven against such people.

First, such people are described in very strong and unpalatable terms in the Scripture—Psalm 14:1 refers to them as fools. Second, according to the Apostle Paul in the text above, they become futile in their thoughts and their hearts became darkened. Thirdly, God removes His restraining hand and gives them up to their uncleanness and the vile passions in their hearts.

This is a heavy price to pay. Satan is on the loose in this world. Mankind cannot afford not to have the hand of God with us for protection or for God to give us up to the passions and lusts in our hearts. The heart, left to its own devices, is desperately wicked and can imagine every vile thing to do to its own detriment. Mankind needs the restraining hand of God on our lives to lead us on the right path for our own good. Man needs enlightened minds to receive light from God in order to be creative and compete in this world. The world is becoming a more and more complex place to live. Our hearts and minds must receive light and wisdom from God in order to be relevant.

Saul of Tarsus was filled with hatred, violence and wickedness against the Christians of his day until a light from heaven shone on him. He later wrote about what love is. When God gives up a man to futile thoughts and a darkened heart, destructive behavior that ruins lives is often the result. We see many such examples around us today; the daily news is always full of people who possess great talent, knowledge, skill and riches, but who are wrecking their own lives with self-destructive behavior. For some of them, God has given them up; so they have become futile in their thoughts and darkened in their hearts. Life without God, our Maker, is a disaster, plain and simple.

Acknowledge God, and He will do unimaginably good things in your life. Acknowledge what the Psalmist wrote: *"Know that the LORD, He is God; It is He who has made us, and not we ourselves; We are His people and the sheep of His pasture. Enter His gates with thanksgiving, and into His courts with praise. Be thankful to Him, and bless His name"* (Psalm 100:3–4).

Some educational systems today teach children that the world came into existence by other means rather than through God. In the process of teaching science and scientific truths to our children, they plant seeds of unbelief in them about God who made the heavens and the earth. In some cases, school children are being brought up to profess that they do not believe in God because of science, and that the universe came into existence by chance instead of being created by God. These lies can be overcome only by a strong practice of faith and worship in the home and in the church, coupled with parents modeling a lifestyle of gratitude and glorifying God. If you are a parent, for the sake of your children you must maintain such a lifestyle to set a good example for your children. This cannot be taken away from them by secular theories taught in school.

One other consequence of being given up by God to vile passions is to have a foolish and darkened heart, which according to Romans 1:26b–27, is to exchange the natural use for what is against nature: *"For even their women exchanged the natural use for what is against nature. Likewise also the men, leaving the natural use of the woman, burned in their lust for one another, men with men committing what is shameful, and receiving in themselves the penalty of their error which was due."* This comes from suppressing the truth about God and refusing to glorify and be thankful to Him.

Around the world, we are pressured to accept homosexuality and lesbianism as a normal choice for society. Many people in this group claim they were born with these desires—man with sexual desire for man and woman with desire for woman. However, Scripture clearly states that this desire is unnatural and comes from vile passions in a darkened heart. Failure to acknowledge God for who He is; to recognize His attributes, eternal power and Godhead; to be thankful to Him results in our darkened hearts being given up by God to uncleanness, lust and dishonor. If you have been struggling with such passions, the way back for you is to start acknowledging God for who He is, learning to glorify Him and being thankful to Him not only for who He is but also for His attributes and eternal power.

Some people do not deny the existence of God; in fact, they profess to believe in Him. They know of Him and do not deny the revelation of God in their hearts. Yet, they do not glorify Him in their lives, neither are they thankful to Him. They don't connect the attributes of God to what is happening in their own lives each day. They are too busy to pause and glorify and thank Him or express gratitude to Him. Although they enjoy His attributes daily, they are like the nine lepers who were cleansed by the Lord Jesus Christ but in a hurry to get their certificates for rehabilitation into society. They are after the benefits of the God who made them, but not a relationship which is characterized by worship and gratitude. Their profession of faith in God is merely mental assent or words; their actions do not show that they acknowledge that God made them. If you really know that God made you, it will be reflected in how you glorify and thank Him. Don't let a day pass without thanking the God who made you and is sustaining you.

Thanksgiving—A Daily Job Profile Under King David

Thanksgiving to God was so important to King David that when he was giving his son Solomon the order of service of the Levites, he asked him to appoint some of the Levitical priests to be solely responsible *"to stand every morning to thank and praise the LORD, and likewise at evening"* (1 Chronicles 23:30). That was their entire job as priests—thanking and praising God every morning and every evening and at every presentation of a burnt offering.

Make thanksgiving to God part of your life every single day, and your life will be transformed. The daily act of thanksgiving will unlock more provision from God's heavenly store into your life.

Chapter Six

Attributes of God that Demand Daily Thanksgiving

"*Through the Lord's mercies we are not consumed, Because His compassions fail not. They are new every morning; Great is Your faithfulness. 'The Lord is my portion,' says my soul, 'Therefore I hope in Him!' The Lord is good to those who wait for Him, To the soul who seeks Him. It is good that one should hope and wait quietly for the salvation of the Lord*" (Lamentations 3:22–26).

God is merciful.

All of us are alive and breathing today because God is merciful. Without His mercies, we should have been consumed by the forces at work in this world. We have all done things knowingly or out of ignorance which could have resulted in death. But because of His mercies, He has pardoned and protected us and kept us alive. David confirmed this in Psalm 103:10-11: "*He has not dealt with us according to our sins, Nor punished us according to our iniquities. For as the heavens are high above the earth, so great is His mercy toward those who fear Him.*"

When we wake from sleep each day, thanksgiving should be on our lips. Every time we return home from work, from the hustle and bustle of the city, town or village in which we live and work, we need to thank Him for preserving us. We could have been consumed during the day by all types of evil forces, accidents or by our own actions. He protects us and gives us another day to live out of His vast store of mercy.

God is compassionate.

Again in Psalm 103, David shows us how God's compassion towards us overrules His judgment or punishment that we deserve. *"As far as the east is from the west, so far has He removed our transgression from us. As a father pities his children, so the* LORD *pities those who fear Him. For He knows our frame; He remembers that we are dust"* (Psalm 103:12–14). His compassion towards us enables Him not to count our sins and transgressions with a legalistic rod of punishment. Instead, it enables Him to be longsuffering towards us and, like the father of the prodigal son, He instead watches for the day when we will repent of our sins and open the door to His forgiveness.

When it comes to temptations, Paul mentioned that God will not allow us to be tempted beyond what we are able to bear. Even with every temptation that comes our way, He will make available the way of escape for us to have victory. As a result of His compassion towards us, He is on our side; He is for us and with us. His attribute of compassion is enough reason to thank Him daily for who He is and how He relates to us.

God is faithful.

God is faithful! *"God is not a man, that He should lie…Has He said, and will He not do? Or has He spoken, and will He not make it good?"* (Numbers 23:19) He is always faithful to His Word, which tells us, *"…it is impossible for God to lie…"* (Hebrews 6:18), and *"…which God, who cannot lie, promised before time began"* (Titus 1:2). The Scripture emphasizes in many places the fact that God is faithful, and He cannot lie or break His promises. It is easy for us to accept that. However, not many people easily realize that they can depend on God's faithfulness. Not many understand that God's faithfulness is benefitting them on a daily basis. If it were not for God's faithfulness in keeping us, we would have been destroyed already. He is holding our lives together despite all the pressures and harassment we face daily in life. The enemy may seek to break us down, yet here we are. *"But the very hairs of your head are all numbered. Do not fear therefore; you are of more value than many sparrows"* (Luke 12:7).

It is proper that we thank Him for His faithfulness with each new day that dawns. He is the One who keeps us alive for His glory. *"He will not allow your foot to be moved; He who keeps you will not slumber. Behold, He who keeps Israel shall neither slumber nor sleep"* (Psalm 121:3–4). When we contrast God's faithfulness towards us with how unfaithful we have been to Him, we have no option but to thank Him and express our gratitude to Him for His attribute of faithfulness. The children of Israel missed out on this one; otherwise, they would have remembered the faithfulness of God to them in the past each time they encountered a new difficulty. They should have encouraged one another that since God had been so faithful to them in the past, always coming through for them, the current problems they were facing would also be temporary. They should have considered that God's faithfulness would not allow Him to leave them without His care.

When dark clouds hang over your head, you must first remember the faithfulness of God and respond to Him with gratitude rather than with fear and complaints. Don't voice the fear even when you are fearful. Don't say you will perish even when you feel you might. Following Paul's example in 2 Corinthians 4:17, consider the dark clouds as light afflictions. They will not crush you, for He is holding your life together by the word of His power.

Secondly, declare your burdens or problems to be temporary afflictions. They are what they are—clouds—and clouds do move on. You can even command them, in the name of the Lord Jesus Christ, to move on.

God is good.

God is good. He is good to those who wait for Him and seek Him. If you have been waiting on Him, He will fill you with good things. *"No good thing will He withhold from those who walk uprightly"* (Psalm 84:11). Everyone has a testimony of good things that have come their way at one time or another which they realize they could never have obtained without God's kindness or favor. It is in God's nature to fill us with good things. *"Every good gift and every perfect gift are from above, and comes down from the Father of lights, with whom there is no variation or shadow of turning"* (James 1:17).

The Scripture also assures us that God is good to everyone on the earth because goodness is His attribute. Psalm 145:9 (NIV) declares, *"The LORD is good to all; he has compassion on all he has made."* He is good to believers as well as those who do not believe in Christ. He allows even unbelievers to share in the blessings He pours out on the earth. *"For He makes His sun rise on the evil and on the good, and sends rain on the just and on the unjust"* (Matthew 5:45b). The whole earth should be rejoicing in God our Maker, thanking Him for His goodness to all men.

His goodness is evidenced by the fact that he draws sinners to repentance from their sins and evil ways. He is inviting them, out of His goodness, to accept His salvation through Christ Jesus, His Son. Are you aware that it is the goodness of the Lord that brings us to repentance? Do you not know that *"the goodness of God leads you to repentance"?* (Romans 2:4b). Because of His goodness to all men, God hears us when we pray for lost souls to be saved. He sent His only begotten Son into the world to hang on the cross and shed His blood for our salvation while we were yet sinners and enemies in our minds against Him. We all have reason to thank Him for His goodness.

Another evidence of His goodness is echoed by David in Psalm 31. *"Oh, how great is Your goodness, which You have laid up for those who fear You, which You have prepared for those who trust in You in the presence of the sons of men! You shall hide them in the secret place of Your* _presence from the plots of man; You shall keep them secretly in a pavilion from the strife of tongues_" (Psalm 31:19–20). The Lord has already laid up stores of His goodness for those who trust in Him in the presence of men. He will protect them in His presence from the plots and strife of evil men. We should thank Him for what He has already prepared and has waiting for us.

You are alive today so that you can see God's goodness in the land of the living. Don't lose heart about your tomorrow or assume that whatever you may be going through today will crush you. David said, "_I would have lost heart, unless I had believed that I would see the goodness of the Lord in the land of the living_" (Psalm 27:13). We have hope for life because of God's goodness. When we know Him well as a good God, we can believe that the future holds good things from Him for us. Instead of despairing of life, we are able to keep on living with hope. For this reason, while we are thankful for His goodness today, we also know that we can thank Him for the goodness He has in store for all of our tomorrows.

God is our salvation.

The angel told Joseph in a dream, "_And she_ [Mary] _will bring forth a Son, and you shall call His name Jesus, for He will save His people from their sins_" (Matthew 1:21). The name Jesus means Yahweh is salvation. Our God is salvation. It is in His nature to save. He likes to save us from our sins, eternal death, danger, the enemy and disasters.

In Ezekiel 33:11, God told the prophet Ezekiel to say to the children of Israel: *"Say to them: 'As I live,' says the Lord God, 'I have no pleasure in the death of the wicked, but that the wicked turn from his way and live. Turn, turn from your evil ways! For why should you die, O house of Israel?'"* The Lord prefers to see the sinner repent and be forgiven rather than be punished for his sins. He puts watchmen in our way to warn us of impending disaster and doom. When we pay heed to the warnings and turn from our wicked ways, He saves us. He does not hold the past against us forever.

"For God so loved the world that He gave His only begotten Son, that whoever believes in Him should not perish but have everlasting life. For God did not send His Son into the world to condemn the world, but that the world through Him might be saved" (John 3:16–17). As we place our faith in the Lord Jesus Christ for salvation, His blood cleanses us and we are reconciled to the Father. We become His sons and daughters and dwell in His protection.

With His overarching desire to save us, we can depend on Him to save us not only from our sins and hell but also from dangers, disasters, perils and the traps of the enemy in this life. He deserves our wholehearted thanks that He is our salvation in so many ways. He is our Savior. In 2 Corinthians 1:10, Paul spoke of Him as the God, *"who delivered us from so great a death, and does deliver us; in whom we trust that He will still deliver us."*

Our gratitude to Him for His salvation in the past gives us the faith to believe that He will save us when we come against problems, perils, dangers and traps laid for us. Knowing Him as *Yahweh is salvation* also enables us to wait on Him quietly for that salvation to manifest. By knowing that He is our salvation, when we come to moments of perplexity or testing, we can wait on Him with confident hope that He will save us from our difficulties. Because of our confidence in His salvation, our response to times of testing will be gratitude from our hearts instead of whining, sulking and questioning God with an attitude of doubt and unbelief.

Those who do not press on to learn about God's attributes, like those espoused by the prophet Jeremiah, find it easy to be glad and rejoice only when they have no immediate needs. But in times of hunger, thirst or lack, their gratitude and thanksgiving fly out of the window and they grumble, murmur or question God due to their unbelief. But His attributes prove Him to be worthy of our sacrifice of praise and thanksgiving every day! The Psalmist reminds us powerfully that, *"It is good to give thanks to the LORD, and to sing praises to Your name, O Most High; To declare Your lovingkindness in the morning, and Your faithfulness every night"* (Psalm 92:1–2).

Thanksgiving to God— Our Priestly Duty

GOD HAS ALWAYS desired a kingdom of priests! One of the sacrifices that believers under the New Covenant are called on to give God is praise. Hebrews 13:15 commands, *"Therefore by Him let us continually offer the sacrifice of praise to God, that is, the fruit of our lips, giving thanks to His name."*

Under the New Covenant, all believers have been made into priests and kings. When Jesus washed us in His blood, He made us kings and priests unto God: *"...to Him who loved us and washed us from our sins in His own blood, and has made us kings and priests to His God"* (Revelation 1:5b–6a).

When God delivered the Israelites out of slavery in Egypt, He expressed His desire for them to be a kingdom of priests and a holy nation (Exodus 19:6). However, the children of Israel failed to fulfil this desire. Anytime they came to any point of difficulty on their journey, they would complain, grumble and murmur to Moses and Aaron. They thought they were angry with Moses and Aaron, but they were indirectly expressing disappointment in God and implying that He was unable to provide for them. They complained and spoke against the Promised Land. On many occasions, they demanded to be taken back to Egypt so they could have their favorite foods like garlic, cucumber, onions, and leeks.

Praising God and giving thanks to His name were far from their hearts and lips. For them to have succeeded in becoming a kingdom of priests and a holy nation, their camp should have been full of praises and thanksgiving unto God. But the mentality they had acquired while in slavery held them captive. They were taken out of Egypt, but they brought that mentality with them. They did not know how to relate to God as His holy nation, a kingdom of priests and therefore an example to other nations. They created a golden calf at one time and worshipped it as the god who delivered them out of Egypt. Consequently, God limited the priesthood to the house of Aaron with the Levitical tribe to help the priests in their duties.

Under the New Covenant, Jesus the Son of God hung on the cross and shed His sinless blood for our redemption. When we place our faith in Him, He redeems us from sin. We have been washed in His blood, which is so powerful that it also cleanses our conscience from dead works. He sanctifies us with His blood. What the children of Israel could not be to the Father when journeying through the wilderness to the Promised Land, Jesus has made us to be under this New Covenant. He has made us kings and priests unto the Father. *"And they sang a new song, saying: 'You are worthy to take the scroll, and to open its seals; For You were slain, and have redeemed us to God by Your blood out of every tribe and tongue and people and nation, and have made us kings and priests to our God; and we shall reign on the earth"* (Revelation 5:9-10).

The fact that we believers are priests unto God under the New Covenant is also brought out clearly by the Apostle Peter in his epistle: *"Coming to Him as to a living stone, rejected indeed by men, but chosen by God and precious, you also, as living stones, are being built up a spiritual house, a holy priesthood, to offer up spiritual sacrifices acceptable to God through Jesus Christ"* (1 Peter 2:5). We are a holy priesthood to God. As priests we are to offer spiritual sacrifices which are acceptable to God. Peter qualified the sacrifices as spiritual and not physical. Under the New Covenant we cannot offer bulls, goats or animals as sacrifices as the priests did under the Old Covenant. For us, our Lord Jesus Christ has made a perfect sacrifice for us once and for all time. He offered Himself as the ransom for our redemption. He was a perfect sacrifice and no physical sacrifice for sins will ever be needed again. The sacrifices that we are called to offer now are spiritual, as stated in the New Testament. These include:

- Presenting our bodies as a living sacrifice (Romans 12:1)
- Giving the sacrifice of praise (Hebrews 13:15)
- The giving of thanks, which is the fruit of our lips (Hebrews 13:15)
- The sharing of our goods with others (Hebrews 13:16)
- Our prayers and intercession (Hebrews 7:25)
- The offering of sacrifices and gifts (Hebrews 5:1)

Many more spiritual sacrifices exist, such as doing good and sharing from Hebrews 13:16; but the main point of that verse is that God is well pleased with such sacrifices.

The children of Israel failed to offer the sacrifice of praise to God while on their journey through the wilderness. Today, we might also have wilderness moments in our lives. How do we respond? Do we respond like the children of Israel, questioning God's ability to protect and keep us and provide for us? The difference between them and us is that we have been washed in the blood of our Lord Jesus Christ, sanctified and made priests and kings to God. We should not live in the realm of complaining, grumbling and murmuring against God during our moments of testing. We should put on the attitude of gratitude even during the hard times.

The key word for us in Hebrews 13:15 should be continually. The verse begins, *"Therefore by Him let us continually offer the sacrifice of praise to God."* At all times, both good and bad, let His praise be upon our lips. Our Lord Jesus Christ has taught us that out of the abundance of the heart the mouth speaks, so that gratitude must first be in our hearts. Our hearts must be grateful to Him for who He is, His attributes, what He has done for us in the past and what He continues to do for us presently. That is why the promise of a new heart under the New Covenant is good news for us. Through our new birth experience, we receive a new heart from the Spirit of the Lord. With this new heart, we can lay aside *"all malice, all deceit, hypocrisy, envy, and all evil speaking"* (1 Peter 2:1) and offer the spiritual sacrifice of continual thanksgiving to God. The Apostle Paul also reiterated this as our lifestyle, duty and God's will for our lives. He urged us to put on the attitude of gratitude to God—thereby fulfilling His will.

"No duty is more urgent than that of returning thanks."

—James Allen

CHAPTER EIGHT

THANKSGIVING TO GOD—
HIS WILL FOR DAILY CONTENTMENT

"*REJOICE ALWAYS, PRAY without ceasing, in everything give thanks; for this is the will of God in Christ Jesus for you*" (1 Thessalonians 5:16–18). The Christian is to be occupied with rejoicing, praying and giving thanks to God. These three disciplines will strengthen the heart of the Christian in both good and bad times.

We naturally rejoice when times are good. For instance, when we win some game or sporting event, we feel gladness and joy because we have been declared winners. When we pass examinations, we feel elated that we have succeeded.

When we go through difficulties, we easily turn to the second exhortation—prayer. We ask God to rescue us or save us from the trials around us or strengthen us to go through them. We remember Psalm 121:1-2 where the Psalmist declared, "*I will lift up my eyes to the hills—from whence comes my help? My help comes from the LORD, who made heaven and earth.*" Praying comes to us easily during times when we realize we need divine help or intervention.

The third part of the three-fold cord is learning to give thanks in everything. With this one, what hits us in the eye and raises questions in us is the *"in everything"* part. In every situation—both in victory and in defeat—Paul's exhortation is that we should always be thankful to the Lord. We should still sing songs of thanksgiving and express our gratitude. It would appear then that as long as we are alive, we have reason to thank Him for what is happening with us, in us and around us every day.

We have seen how considering the five attributes of God that Jeremiah outlined in Lamentations 3:22–25 should lead us to a lifestyle of gratitude and thanksgiving. We can also find reasons other than His attributes to let our lives flow with ceaseless praise and thanksgiving to Him as commanded in the New Testament. These reasons revolve around what He does for us.

REASON ONE:
He has given us the gift of His Son, Jesus Christ.

The ultimate gift that God has given to the world is His Son, our Lord Jesus Christ. Through Him we have received redemption from our sins as well as from the punishment of eternal death and hell. Jesus Christ in our hearts is the gift of God to us.

Before we even consider other gifts we receive from God, this gift should evoke in us thanksgiving to God without ceasing. Through Him, we are able to receive a new and abundant life from the Father. By Him, our sins can be forgiven and the power of sin in our lives can be broken. Our nature can be changed from sinners to saints. We can be made the righteousness of God in Christ Jesus. When we accept that gift, we become righteousness-conscious instead of sin-conscious. We have been redeemed from the clutches of Satan and all his oppression on the earth. Christ has given us authority over all his powers; and we are to reign on earth because of the abundance of God's grace and by His gift of righteousness. We are certain we will spend eternity with Christ Jesus and not be doomed to hell. In short, we have been delivered and translated from the kingdom of darkness into God's kingdom of light. All these have happened to us because God gave us His Son, Jesus Christ, to come and save us by offering His life as a sacrifice on the cross for us. God gave His Son for this purpose because He loves us.

We cannot ever stop thanking Him for our salvation and all its tremendous benefits. As part of this salvation, we have healing from sicknesses and diseases and are entitled to live in health, prosperity and peace. God's peace is not only the absence of stress or conflicts but also includes divine health, well-being, wholeness, and prosperity. Hebrews 6:9 says, *"But, beloved, we are confident of better things concerning you, yes, things that accompany salvation, though we speak in this manner."* When we remember our former life before we came to Christ Jesus and consider the new life we enjoy in Him and the benefits of our salvation, we cannot stop thanking Him. Words are not adequate to express the gratitude we should feel in our hearts for Him.

As we thank Him like the one healed leper who returned, the door to more of the things in the "package" that accompanies salvation will be unlocked to us. We receive more from His bounty as a result of our thanksgiving for the "healing" or cleansing from the "leprosy" of sin. Like the leper who returned with gratitude, we begin to enjoy wholeness from the lifestyle of gratitude and thanksgiving for our salvation.

In Ephesians 5:19-20, Paul admonishes us to be *"speaking to one another in psalms and hymns and spiritual songs, singing and making melody in your heart to the Lord, giving thanks always for all things to God the Father in the name of our Lord Jesus Christ."* To the Christian, every day should be a day of ceaseless thanksgiving to God for the gift of His Son, the Lord Jesus Christ, who saved us and gave us eternal life. *"Thanks be to God for His indescribable gift"* (2 Corinthians 9:15).

REASON TWO:
He gives us good and perfect gifts.

James 1:17 says, *"Every good gift and every perfect gift is from above, and comes down from the Father of lights, with whom there is no variation or shadow of turning."* God is a giver. He gives to us, His children, because He loves us. Since there is no variation or darkness in Him, the gifts He gives to us are good and perfect.

First, we must open our arms to receive His gifts willingly and with delight. Secondly, since His gifts are good and perfect, we should respond with appreciation, gratitude and thankfulness to Him.

REASON THREE:
He gives us daily benefits.

In addition to the indescribable gift of His Son Jesus Christ, God is always lavishing us with gifts. Everything we have in this world is a gift from God. The very breath in us is a gift from God; without it, we will pass on into the next life according to Scripture: *"For as the body without the spirit is dead"* (James 2:26a). Without breath, lifeless bodies are buried in the grave and covered with dirt by loved ones, friends and family. Or, they are cremated—burnt to ashes. David understood this well, and in many of his psalms he sang, *"As long as I have breath in me, I will praise my Maker."* Even when we find ourselves in difficulties and moments of lack and deprivation such as the children of Israel sometimes experienced in their journey through the wilderness, we must still thank God for the gift of life. We cannot take it for granted. It is only by His mercy and compassion that we are alive today.

The Psalmist in Psalm 68:19-20a also reminds us that in addition to being alive, He still loads us with other benefits: *"Blessed be the LORD, who daily loads us with benefits, the God of our salvation. Selah. Our God is the God of salvation"* (Psalm 68:19).

He gives us what we need on daily basis, and this daily benevolence may cause some to take His generosity for granted. We do this so much that we fail to appreciate and thank Him for them. This is what we saw in the children of Israel. Every day they were collecting manna from the fields. This was a supernatural provision for their daily bread. It was miraculous considering that it was falling from heaven. The Psalmist alluded to this manna as angels' food in Psalm 78:24–25. God was so faithful in His provision for forty years that there was never a time when the manna did not fall from heaven for the Israelites.

Logically, you would have thought that, when they came to a place when there was no water, they would have believed that the God who provided them with manna so miraculously and faithfully would also provide them with water in His own miraculous way. But this was so far from their minds because they had gotten to the place where they took the manna for granted. It no longer moved them. Its awe had been lost on them. Thus, they yearned for new provision without remembering the past provisions and faithfulness of God.

Today, when we too come to a place or a time of lack in our lives, we should look at the daily provisions God has been supplying for us and have faith that He will still provide. His daily provisions may appear mundane to us, but they point to God's faithfulness and should not be lost on us. Our current need and testing should not blind us so that we fail to appreciate that God is our daily Provider. We can still thank Him in every circumstance, whether supply is available or not. Paul, like Moses, is appropriately instructing us that we should give thanks in everything, for this is the will of God in Christ Jesus for us.

IN EVERYTHING GIVE THANKS

WE HAVE DEALT with what is required of us during moments of lack, need, and deprivation. We saw that during such times, instead of leaning on God, the children of Israel engaged in speaking evil and malice against God. We saw their inability to cultivate a heart of gratitude based on their past experience with God and the resultant ingratitude they showed Him. We have discussed how to counteract such ingratitude in our lives.

It is not only when we face lack or a need or when we are deprived that we are challenged to be thankful. Troubles, storms and disasters can come against us and threaten to overwhelm us or leave us perplexed and wearied. They can come in such a way that we are left panting for breath, confused and fighting for survival. On many occasions, we ask ourselves why trouble or disaster is befalling us. We wonder why God allows us to go through certain problems in life. During such times, we are driven to prayer, seeking the face of God for His intervention.

> "Thankfulness is the beginning of gratitude. Gratitude is the completion of thankfulness. Thankfulness may consist merely of words. Gratitude is shown in acts."
>
> – H. F. Amiel

While we are asking for His intervention, He still expects us to be thankful. We must show gratitude during such perplexities. In fact, He wants us to thank Him when we are right in the middle of such situations. He wants us to stop asking why and start thanking Him.

At other times, our difficulty could be people we meet and deal with in life who are treating us unfairly or badly, causing deep hurt. We might feel like complaining or cursing such people, but Paul still admonished us to give thanks to God in everything. God has commanded us not to take offence or complain or be bitter; instead of self-pity, we are to be thankful during unfair treatment and adverse circumstances. If we do not pay heed to God's prescription for a solution, we can easily become perplexed and confused by unfair treatment. The solution from God is to remain thankful and show gratitude to God for His numerous blessings. We may not feel like thanking Him when the heat is on, but that is the only way to overcome the hurt and pain of such situations.

> "The more I look at the times thanks is mentioned in God's Word, the more I notice...This giving of thanks has nothing to do with my circumstances and everything to do with my God."
> –Jenni Hunt

By the way, the three-fold instruction in 1 Thessalonians 5:17–19—rejoice always, pray without ceasing and in everything give thanks—is intertwined. These three disciplines should always be ongoing in our lives since each one feeds and fuels the others. They do not exist or work effectively in isolation. If you are thankful to God, you will also rejoice in Him; if you are prayerful, you can thank Him even when the situations around you are not favorable. If you are rejoicing always, you have the faith to go to Him in prayer more than ever. When you have learned to rejoice in the Lord and are prayerful, however severe the pressure or difficult the situation, you are still able to give thanks to the Lord in everything. You will avoid the incessant complaints, murmuring and grumbling that the children of Israel resorted to in the wilderness on their way to the Promised Land. Remember that they all died in the wilderness as a result of their ingratitude, complaints, and disobedience to God. An attitude of rejoicing in the Lord always, prayerfulness, and giving thanks to God in every situation will strengthen and help you reach your God-ordained destiny. As a matter of fact, when we give thanks to God in adversity, God moves speedily into our situation to show forth His presence, power and deliverance. Paul was teaching not only what should be, but what had been his practice and means of receiving divine strength and experiencing God's supernatural deliverance.

Thanksgiving Always, Even in Challenging Situations

It was in Philippi that Paul exemplified this by showing that this was indeed his lifestyle. He and Silas cast out a spirit of divination from a young slave girl who was following them for days and distracting people from their preaching. You would have thought that bringing deliverance to a demon-possessed girl would be appreciated by the townsfolk. Ironically, Paul and Silas were instead flogged mercilessly and thrown into jail. The magistrates *"...commanded them to be beaten with rods. And when they had laid many stripes on them, they threw them into prison, commanding the jailer to keep them securely. Having received such a charge, he put them into the inner prison and fastened their feet in the stocks"* (Acts 16:22–24).

Everything about this experience seemingly provided grounds for being perplexed and complaining against God. Paul and Silas were led to Philippi by the Spirit of God. Initially, they had wanted to visit Bithynia, but the Spirit of God had not permitted them. The Spirit led them to Macedonia instead, and they thus came to the city of Philippi in Macedonia where they found themselves in jail after having been beaten severely. To top it off, they were thrown into the inner prison, the most secure place, presumably among the hardened criminals. In addition to that, their feet were bound in stocks. Many people in Philippi who were possessed with unclean and demonic spirits would have been looking for genuine men of God (like Paul and Silas) to minister deliverance to them, but could not find any. Then these two authentic men of God ministered the grace of God and brought peace to a vulnerable young girl who had been held a slave for gain by her master, and their reward was being beaten with rods and thrown into jail among the hardened criminals with their feet bound in stocks.

Had Paul and Silas possessed the attitude of the children of Israel, they would have called on the Spirit of God to take them back to "Egypt" (or, in Paul and Silas's case, to Antioch) immediately. They would have grumbled and murmured that to be in their comfort zone in Antioch (where Paul was sent out from) was better than going on a missionary journey.

Christians today would have called down fire on the owners of the slave girl, the magistrates, and all of the townsfolk who rose up to beat Paul and Silas. But Paul and Silas responded very differently. Though they found themselves maltreated, beaten unjustly without a proper trial, and imprisoned among hardened criminals, their response was quite different: *"But at midnight Paul and Silas were praying and singing hymns to God, and the prisoners were listening to them. Suddenly there was a great earthquake, so that the foundations of the prison were shaken; and immediately all the doors were opened and everyone's chains were loosed"* (Acts 16:25-26).

Paul and Silas prayed and sang hymns to God, and they weren't quiet about it! Nor were they sorrowful. If they had been, the prisoners would not have bothered to listen to them because they were accustomed to seeing those thrown into prison unjustly express sorrow. However, Paul and Silas had a different attitude and spirit which arrested the attention of the other prisoners. They gave thanks to God for their situation, and their prayer and thanksgiving led to praises.

Thanksgiving to God always leads to singing His praises. When our hearts are genuinely full of gratitude and we are expressing it to God, we sometimes reach a point where words no longer seem adequate to express the depths of our gratitude. Like David, we break forth into song at that point—it's simply another level of communication with our dear Savior. Paul and Silas were rejoicing as they sang hymns of praise in that prison!

The prisoners weren't the only ones who took notice. Where there is sincere gratitude, thanksgiving, rejoicing and prayer, God is always drawn to that scene. The Psalmist said in Psalm 22:3 that God is *"enthroned in the praises of Israel."* Our praises constitute a throne for God. He comes into the midst of the praises of His people to take His place on the throne. That is what Paul and Silas did in the midst of suffering unfair treatment, injustice, and physical pain in prison. Are we also able to do that today? When we pay heed to Paul's admonition—giving thanks to God in everything—our thanksgiving attracts God into our situation. Thanksgiving or gratitude opens the door to that realm in which the presence of God manifests strongly around us.

How do we know that God was drawn to their situation in the prison? We see that while Paul and Silas were praising God, an earthquake shook the very foundations of the prison; all the prison doors were immediately opened, and everyone's chains were loosed. God's presence entered that prison, and all the prisoners in that jail were loosed immediately! Those other prisoners benefitted from God showing up in response to the praises of Paul and Silas.

The lesson is this: Paul and Silas's ability to keep their hearts and mouths from complaining and grumbling about unfair treatment and choosing gratitude, rejoicing and praise to God instead invited God into their situation with such manifested glory that the doors of their prison opened of their own accord. God is the same yesterday, today and forevermore. Your attitude of gratitude to Him, which leads to praises from a rejoicing spirit, can open every door to set you free from the prison of bitterness and complaints owing to unfair treatment. When God's presence entered that jail, He was after not only the doors but the chains too. Every chain holding you bound in life can be broken!

We will all inevitably experience unfair treatment from other people in this life. Misunderstanding, injustice, enslavement, being repaid with evil for the good that we do to others—all are common occurrences here on earth. It is how we respond to these events that determines the length of our suffering. Consequently, Paul is teaching us that, from heaven's perspective, unceasing prayer, rejoicing and thankfulness to God always provide the key to our freedom. God is drawn into our situation by these three disciplines; and when He is in our midst, chains are broken, prison doors are opened, and we can go forward in life to our next level. As we saw earlier, without the attitude of gratitude, the children of Israel kept looking back to Egypt until they died in the wilderness. May the Lord help each of us to always have the grace to put on the attitude of gratitude.

Though they refused to leave the prison after the earthquake that loosed their chains, Paul and Silas were eventually taken out of the jail in Philippi. The jailer took them to his house, set food before them and treated them with dignity, respect and honor. He dressed their wounds and sought to know how he, too, could be saved and experience the presence of God in his life in a powerful way. Paul and Silas led the jailer and his household to the Lord Jesus Christ before returning to the prison. The next morning, the magistrates came personally to plead with Paul & Silas when they learned they were Roman citizens and should therefore have been fairly tried before being imprisoned, and they ended up escorting the two men out of the prison with respect and fear. When God turns situations around for you, there is no end to what He does to elevate His children to their rightful place. He only requires that we are dependent on Him with the right attitude to create the right atmosphere for Him to intervene in our case. That is what the three-fold attitude of rejoicing, gratitude and prayer can achieve for you.

Paul was thrown into jail again in Rome about AD 61. From prison, he wrote a beautiful epistle to the church in Philippi. His epistle was full of encouragement to Christians to be joyful. He exuded joy. Though his condition in the prison was not convenient, Paul still found reasons to be grateful and positive about his imprisonment as well as thankful to God. Paul wrote to the Philippian church: *"But I want you to know, brethren, that the things which happened to me have actually turned out for the furtherance of the gospel, so that it has become evident to the whole palace guard, and to all the rest, that my chains are in Christ; and most of the brethren in the Lord, having become confident by my chains, are much more bold to speak the word without fear"* (Philippians 1:12-14).

Instead of complaining about his chains and the discomfort of imprisonment, Paul instead referred to *"the things which happened to me"* (his imprisonment) as furthering the gospel. He was imprisoned for preaching the gospel of the Lord Jesus Christ, so how did his imprisonment advance the cause of the gospel? He started with the palace guards, who were many in number. As they took turns guarding him, Paul would witness to them about the Lord Jesus Christ. One by one, they were converted to Christianity—the very reason Paul was in jail. Instead of whining over his plight of imprisonment, he used his imprisonment for the cause of Christ. He accepted the pain of imprisonment as part of his proclamation of the gospel and was rejoicing in the results. Paul recognized a second positive outcome of his imprisonment when he noted that other Christians had become bolder in preaching the gospel of Jesus Christ without fear. Paul made no room in his heart for complaining, grumbling, bitterness and feeling sorry for himself. Instead, he looked upward with gratitude for the outcomes he was seeing.

What a good lesson! When faced with adverse conditions, unfair treatment, injustice and misunderstanding, we must make no room in our hearts for complaining and bitterness. Secondly, we need to look at the outcome of the situation or how the situation affects the cause of Christ. Like Paul, once we see the positive results from our situation, we can also express joy at our negative or adverse circumstances and be thankful to God in everything.

When we choose to respond with thankfulness, we will appreciate more than ever the notable verse that says, *"And we know that all things work together for good to those who love God, to those who are the called according to His purpose"* (Romans 8:28). Then we are empowered to thank and praise Him in the midst of fiery trials and unpleasant situations.

Looking to the Future with Gratitude to God

To the church in Ephesus, Paul later wrote this: "*...singing and making melody in your heart to the Lord, giving thanks always for all things to God the Father in the name of our Lord Jesus Christ*" (Ephesians 5:19b–20). I ought to give thanks always for all things to God the Father in the name of our Lord Jesus Christ? What about when I am hurting? This command to give thanks always for everything was preceded by the command to be filled with the Spirit. That is a vital key to maintaining a tongue of thanksgiving in every situation. The Scripture says when we are filled with His Holy Spirit, our hearts should be in readiness to be in fellowship with others. During these moments of fellowship, we should be speaking to one another not with complaints and lamentations, but with songs, hymns, and psalms. Due to the presence of the Holy Spirit in us, we are enabled to make melody in our hearts to the Lord. From the inspiration of the Spirit who dwells in us, we can give thanks to the Father in every situation and for all things.

The presence of the Holy Spirit in us changes the equation for us. The children of Israel had the Spirit of God working among them, but He was not in them. It was only after Christ came and left us that the Holy Spirit was poured upon us. Now He dwells in us individually and corporately. Therefore, with His indwelling Presence, no matter how much we hurt from adverse situations around us, regardless of the pressure exerted on our flesh to cry, complain and lament, we can still look up to our heavenly Father and give Him thanks first and foremost.

Despite present hurtful circumstances, He holds the future in His loving hands. In fact, He holds our future in His hands: *"And I give them eternal life, and they shall never perish; neither shall anyone snatch them out of My hand"* (John 10:28). Therefore, we can thank Him as we look to the future. We can thank Him now, before the future comes, knowing that He is working all things for our good. We can thank Him because we know that He will deliver us. In the face of risky and near-death situations, Paul appropriately declared. *"Yes, we had the sentence of death in ourselves, that we should not trust in ourselves but in God who raises the dead, who delivered us from so great a death, and does deliver us; in whom we trust that He will still deliver us"* (2 Corinthians 1:9–10). With this level of trust that He will still deliver us, we can rest in Him and freely thank Him today even in hurtful situations.

Paul's Lifestyle of Thanksgiving

Paul's exemplary lifestyle of thanksgiving to God is clear from all the epistles he sent to the churches. He opened almost all of his thirteen epistles with thanksgiving to God. Below are those expressions of thanks to God in the books of the Bible that he penned:

- *"First, I thank my God through Jesus Christ for you all, that your faith is spoken of throughout the whole world"* (Romans 1:8).
- *"I thank my God always concerning you for the grace of God which was given to you by Christ Jesus"* (1 Corinthians 1:4).

- *"Blessed be the God and Father of our Lord Jesus Christ, the Father of mercies and God of all comfort"* (2 Corinthians 1:3).

- *"Blessed be the God and Father of our Lord Jesus Christ, who has blessed us with every spiritual blessing in the heavenly places in Christ"* (Ephesians 1:3).

- *"I thank my God upon every remembrance of you, always in every prayer of mine, making request for you all with joy"* (Philippians 1:3).

- *"We give thanks to the God and Father of our Lord Jesus Christ, praying always for you"* (Colossians 1:3).

- *"We give thanks to God always for you all, making mention of you in our prayers"* (1 Thessalonians 1:2).

- *"We are bound to thank God always for you, brethren, as it is fitting, because your faith grows exceedingly, and the love of every one of you all abounds toward each other"* (2 Thessalonians 1:3).

- *"And I thank Christ Jesus our Lord who has enabled me, because He counted me faithful, putting me into the ministry"* (1 Timothy 1:12).

- *"I thank God, whom I serve with a pure conscience, as my forefathers did, as without ceasing I remember you in my prayers night and day"* (2 Timothy 1:3).

- *"I thank my God, making mention of you always in my prayers"* (Philemon 1:4).

Out of his thirteen epistles, Paul opened eleven of them with thanksgiving for various reasons. It was almost a law for him not to address the churches without first giving thanks to the Father, either for the faith of the people to whom he was writing or for the blessings of God upon them. His epistles were warm, and the thanksgiving he expressed to God was sincere.

This is a challenging example for us to follow today. Our thanksgiving should arise from our deep appreciation of God and what He has done for us, continues to do and that which we trust Him to do for us in the future. As Paul wrote to the church in Philippi, he was confident that He who had begun a good work in them would complete it until the day of Jesus Christ or until the return of the Lord Jesus Christ. For that reason, thanksgiving to God should always be on our lips, first as a discipline and secondly from our deep appreciation of God and His work in our lives.

Just as Paul opened every epistle with thanksgiving to God, we can open each day with thanksgiving to God, acknowledging that it is by His compassion, mercies, faithfulness and goodness that we have entered a new day. As we saw in Psalm 92, the Psalmist called us to declare His lovingkindness in the morning and His faithfulness in the evening. Start every day with thanksgiving to God!

Chapter Ten

Eight Benefits from a Lifestyle of Thanksgiving

From the examples we have examined so far, we can identify some of the benefits that a lifestyle of gratitude and thanksgiving in every situation brings into our lives.

1) Thanksgiving brings us into God's presence.

The one leper who postponed his journey to the priest and returned to the Lord Jesus to give thanks ended up receiving more than just physical healing from leprosy. First, his thankfulness brought him back into the presence of the Lord Jesus Christ. The nine lepers who were dutifully racing to the priest's house missed the opportunity to have close physical communion with Jesus. In Luke 17, when the lepers first saw Jesus, they shouted to Him from a distance to have mercy on them. They weren't allowed to approach Him and the crowd because of their leprosy. *"Then as He entered a certain village, there met Him ten men who were lepers, who stood afar off. And they lifted up their voices and said, 'Jesus, Master, have mercy on us!'"* (Luke 17:12–13)

However, that one leper who returned came right to where Jesus was and fell down at His feet, giving Him thanks. He experienced a close encounter, in Jesus' physical space, at His feet. The same is true for us today. Being thankful brings us closer to the One whom we are thanking; in fact, it brings us right into the presence of God in the spiritual realm. It always does. Communicating the gratitude we feel in our heart demands that we draw closer to God. That gives us the benefit of being in His presence, and we know from Psalm 16:11 that in His presence is the fulness of joy.

The intentional act of coming into the presence of the Lord Jesus was demonstrated by two women in the New Testament who broke protocol in order to thank the Lord Jesus Christ. In Luke 7:36–39, a woman known in the city as someone who lived a sinful life entered a Pharisee's house uninvited where a meal was being served for Jesus. She washed Jesus' feet with her tears, wiped them with her hair, kissed them in worship, and anointed them with a fragrant oil. Though she hadn't been invited to the lunch, she made up her mind to come into Jesus' presence and thank Him. It was intentional on her part.

When she was being criticized by the Pharisee, Jesus mounted a strong defense of her actions of thanksgiving even though she had entered the house uninvited. Jesus said she had so much affection and passion in her thanksgiving and worship because she had been forgiven much. *"Therefore I say to you, her sins, which are many, are forgiven, for she loved much. But to whom little is forgiven, the same loves little.' Then Jesus said to her, 'Your sins are forgiven… your faith has saved you. Go in peace'"* (Luke 7:47-48, 50).

Just as the Lord Jesus commended the one leper who returned to give thanks, He commended this woman for drawing near to Him and thanking and worshipping Him. These commendations from Jesus endorsed their drawing close to Him to give thanks.

Just as in the natural or physical realm, the thanks-giver has to physically come close to the Lord Jesus to express gratitude for what He had done, our expressions of gratitude to God attract a drawing or a pull from God in the spiritual realm. God draws us closer to Himself. The more we thank Him, the more we sense Him drawing us closer to Himself in a sweet communion or time of fellowship. We experience His peace when we thank Him. He draws us closer to Himself, beyond the wagging tongues of criticism from onlookers and condemnation from even ourselves. Be a thanks-giver, and your back will be well covered by the Lord before others.

2) Thanksgiving fulfils divine protocol for entry into His presence.

Psalm 100:4-5 says, *"Enter into His gates with thanksgiving, and into His courts with praise. Be thankful to Him, and bless His name. For the Lord is good; His mercy is everlasting, and His truth endures to all generations."* Thanksgiving is God's prescribed protocol for entry into His Presence. Just like the gratitude felt by the leper and the forgiven woman brought them close to Jesus so they could express their thanksgiving in the physical world, when we lift up our voices in thanksgiving, wherever we are, we are fulfilling His requirement for entry into

His courts. Thanksgiving opens the door for us to enter His presence and commune further with Him.

A congregation that focuses on thanksgiving, praises and worship experiences the presence of God in their services more than those who spend little time giving thanks to God. Thus, thanksgiving leads us into a deeper relationship with God, the Giver of our blessings. This is what the nine lepers, racing to the priest's house after they noticed their healing, missed—a relationship with the Giver of their blessing. As Christian author A. W. Tozer asserts, "What is wrong with Christians today is that we have the gifts of God but have forgotten the God of gifts."

Many Christians today still behave like the nine lepers. They have been healed of their leprosy (sin) alright; they are even rejoicing with delight over their forgiveness of sins, which is a good thing to do. However, instead of deepening their relationship with the Giver through gratitude and thanksgiving, they are running away and looking for the next level of blessing. Are you among the nine or are you the one who returned to give thanks?

3) Thanksgiving leads to praise.

When it becomes our lifestyle to continually give thanks to God, praising God is a natural progression. Our lips will not be sealed if we have a grateful heart and express that gratitude continually. Praising God also gives us the advantage of experiencing more of His divine presence. The atmosphere around us changes to a joyful, liberated one. Heavy and oppressive clouds lift as we thank and praise Him. Praise also enables us to engage in spiritual warfare when necessary. Psalm 22:3 says, *"But You are holy, enthroned in the praises of Israel."*

4) Thanksgiving brings us to the realm of wholeness.

What else did that one grateful leper's expression of gratitude to the Lord bring to him as a benefit? First, he had a second meeting with the Lord Jesus Christ. There is no other record in the Bible that the other nine lepers ever met the Lord Jesus Christ again after they were healed. The moment arrives in every situation when our hearts should be pumping with gratitude, and the expression of gratitude must follow. The leper who returned grasped that moment when he realized that he had been healed. His decision to return resulted in the blessing of a second meeting with the Lord Jesus Christ.

Secondly, Jesus took notice of him and even remarked that he was a Samaritan. Thanksgiving will cause you to be noticed by the Lord Jesus Christ. Among the crowd of needy and hurting people seeking His touch and miracles, the Lord Jesus really notices those who come to Him with grateful hearts and are willing to express their gratitude to Him. So many only want the miracles and depart as soon as they have them. Don't be one who accepts the miracles and then runs away from God. Have a grateful heart for what He does and has done for us.

Thirdly, when the one leper returned to express gratitude, Jesus blessed him further with wholeness. Jesus said to him, *"Arise, go your way. Your faith has made you whole."* Wholeness for a leper implied that there was no longer any evidence of leprosy, either active or cured. The other nine lepers were cured all right, but they were still considered as cured or healed lepers. This leper who expressed gratitude was made whole in every sense of the word. New skin was restored to his body, and it was no longer possible to discern that he had once been leprous.

When the Syrian general was healed in 2 Kings 5:1–19, the Scripture records in verse 14, *"…and his flesh was restored like the flesh of a little child, and he was clean."* That was wholeness for the Syrian general. Being made whole went beyond just being healed or cured from leprosy, but wholeness follows gratitude. Your expressions of gratitude to God will bring further blessings, such as being made whole, into your life. The ten lepers cried out to the Lord Jesus, and the door of healing opened to them. One out of the ten lepers made giving thanks his priority, and the door of being made whole was opened only to him as a result. He was made whole because of his attitude of gratitude.

Gratitude is like a key to the heart of God that unlocks doors of provision for us. When Peter was locked up in Herod's prison, the church cried out in prayer without ceasing. Herod's prison doors opened for Peter to come out without the guards' knowledge. When Paul and Silas prayed, gave thanks and praised God in the Philippian jail, not only did the prison doors open, but they were brought to the jailer's house for a meal and accorded honor and dignity before being escorted out of prison by the magistrates. In response to their gratitude, many doors were unlocked for them.

More doors in God's warehouse of provision are waiting to open in response to our consistently maintaining an attitude of gratitude.

Today, many Christians still lack many of God's benefits and blessings that come along with salvation or our redemption. They go through life full of discontent as they stand outside God's warehouse of provision hollering for the blessings that have been provided and stored in God's warehouse for them. Well, the one grateful leper is shouting back to us (through this book) that the key to open the door is to be thankful and express gratitude. It is up to us to use this key in order to see His limitless blessings poured out upon us. Without a lifestyle that prioritizes thanksgiving and gratitude, God's supply of wholeness may be available in Jesus, but we will be racing away from Him, just like the nine lepers did—healed but not made whole.

5) Thanksgiving and praise bring God into your situation.

While God draws you to Himself and covers your back when you are thanking Him, your thanksgiving and praise also bring God right into your situation. When Paul and Silas were in the Philippian jail, wounded and in chains, as they expressed thanks and praise, the presence of God manifested strongly right in their jail.

Not only were they set free and taken care of, but their story of disappointment, perplexity and shame also changed. They were accorded honor and dignity. It is the same today when we decide to look beyond the hurtful situations around us and open our hearts to thank and praise God. Our pain and hurt will soon turn to honor and dignity.

The resilience that Paul showed in the Roman prison is amazing. He had every reason to complain. This man who, as a result of thanksgiving and praises to God, caused an earthquake in the prison in Philippi, who saw God move in supernaturally and set him and the other prisoners free, found himself imprisoned in Rome. Undoubtedly, he thanked God in this situation and praised Him as always; but this time there was no earthquake. His epistle to the Philippian

> "Anybody can thank God for good things. But when you can thank God even in the bad things, your faith grows, and your spiritual roots go deeper."
> — Rick Warren

church from this jail revealed his frame of mind. Reading through the whole epistle, we note that he was instead focused on the joy of his salvation. The whole epistle was a message on joy and rejoicing.

From his prison cell, he was admonishing those who were not in prison to rejoice always. He did not complain about being in jail, nor did he suggest that God had let him down by not responding to his praises in the same way He had done in the Philippian prison. He didn't whine. The epistle opened with his usual words of thanksgiving to God and continued and ended on a joyous note. Undoubtedly, his lifestyle of thanking God in every situation helped him to be focused on God and not on his miserable situation in prison. Gratitude and thanksgiving give inner strength that enables us to take our eyes off the misery around us and focus on what God is doing for us.

6) Thanksgiving to God brings us contentment.

Writing to the Philippians from his dark prison cell, Paul explained that he was content. *"I know how to be abased, and I know how to abound. Everywhere and in all things I have learned both to be full and to be hungry, both to abound and to suffer need. I can do all things through Christ who strengthens me"* (Philippians 4:12-13).

A lifestyle of gratitude and thanksgiving leads to contentment in every situation. Our expression of gratitude to God has the innate power to provide not only strength but also contentment—a heart satisfied and at peace with God. We become content in the Lord when we give Him thanks.

What, then, do we do about our present and future needs? How do we handle the realities of present-day economic hardships, scarcity and pressing needs that may from time to time be staring us in the face? Knowing the benefits of a lifestyle of gratitude and thanksgiving compared to the damage caused by complaints, unbelief and murmuring against God, Paul admonished us not to give in to anxiety over what we need. *"Be anxious for nothing, but in everything by prayer and supplication, with thanksgiving, let your requests be made known to God; and the peace of God, which surpasses all understanding, will guard your hearts and minds through Christ Jesus"* (Philippians 4:6–7).

Just like Moses taught the children of Israel, we can overcome anxieties, fretting, complaining and murmuring with the simple virtue of thanksgiving. Even our requests to God must be accompanied by or undergirded with thanksgiving as we remember that He has delivered us in the past, does deliver today and will continue to deliver us in the times to come. In times of His provision, we thank Him; but in times of need, we still are to thank Him. Thanksgiving to Him should be our daily lifestyle.

Ordinarily, it is not easy to thank God when we face severe needs in life. Our flesh is anxious, and our natural tendency is to cry out to God for His urgent help. During those times when we are more driven to pour out our hearts to Him, we must have a firm faith that God will supply all our need in order to be able to thank Him while our needs still exist. He is our Provider; when we view God in the right perspective, our hearts will be settled that He will surely provide for us. Due to that certainty, we can shirk off the anxieties and lift our voices to thank Him for who He is, what He has done for us in the past, and what He is going to do for us in the future.

An active faith and trust in God should help us always abound with thanksgiving to God.

7) Thanksgiving brings God satisfaction.

As parents, we take pleasure in providing for our households and giving gifts to our children. We find satisfaction when our children are excited about gifts we bring when we return from a journey or simply come home from work at the end of the day. Some children will collect the gift and run away with the excitement or immediately rip into the package. We watch them with pleasure as they unwrap whatever we have given them, but our satisfaction and delight soar when they turn around and say, "Thank you!" When a child thanks his earthly parent for a gift, the parent is satisfied and pleased by that simple act of thanksgiving, and it strengthens the relationship between parent and child.

Similarly, our heavenly Father will derive satisfaction and pleasure from us when we lift up our eyes and thank Him for the gifts He gives us. He is a Giver—He loves to give to us. We have already seen the testimony of King David, in Psalm 68:19, that He loads us daily with benefits. Therefore, if we become the type of children who thank our Father for His gifts, we will bring satisfaction and delight to Him.

In many households, when a child does not offer thanks for a gift, parents call the child back and instruct him to express his gratitude. As that action is repeated each time a child fails to give thanks, the child eventually learns not to take gifts for granted; instead, he develops a habit of expressing gratitude to the giver. May the information in this book be a tool in the hands of the Lord to wake us up to a lifestyle of thanksgiving and expression of our heartfelt gratitude to our God.

8) Thanksgiving releases power for miracles.

The Lord Jesus was with a great multitude of people who had been listening to His teaching for the whole day. Before sunset, He and His disciples knew that the people needed food as they had not eaten all day long. The disciples were overwhelmed with the magnitude of what faced them—how to feed a crowd of over five thousand men, women and children. Philip told the Lord Jesus that even a year's wages (200 denarii) could not buy bread for every one of them. Andrew then spotted a young lad with five barley loaves and two small fish and mentioned it to the Lord Jesus. Before Jesus could even respond, Andrew pointed out the hopelessness of the situation when he asked Jesus in verse 8, *"But what are they among so many?"*

But Jesus asked for the multitude to be organized into small groups of fifty, ready to receive food. Then He gave thanks to the Father and began to distribute the five loaves of bread to the twelve disciples. Those five loaves of bread and two fishes began to multiply in the hands of the disciples, and we see in John 6:11, *"And Jesus took the loaves, and when He had given thanks, He distributed them to the disciples, and the disciples to those sitting down; and likewise of the fish, as much as they wanted."* Jesus' prayer that led to the multiplication of the bread and fish was one of thanksgiving. He responded to the overwhelming need for food for five thousand people (and that didn't include any of the women and children) with thanksgiving to the Father. He did not feel crushed by the weight of the need. He was not overwhelmed; He did not complain about why the multitude had not brought their own food like the young lad. Instead, He resorted to thanking the Father in the face of the need to feed what could have been more than fifteen thousand people. God's power to multiply resources was released to operate in Jesus' hands by thanksgiving.

Again, when Jesus stood by the grave of Lazarus who had been buried four days earlier, He was faced with the task of reversing the power of death and bringing Lazarus back to life. When He needed power to cancel the sting of death in Lazarus' body, Jesus resorted to thanksgiving to the Father. *"Then they took away the stone from the place where the dead man was lying. And Jesus lifted up His eyes and said, 'Father, I thank You that You have heard Me. And I know that You always hear Me'"* (John 11:41-42a). Then He commanded Lazarus to come forth from the grave, and Lazarus, who was bound with grave-clothes, came out from the tomb. He was raised from the dead back to life. The power to raise Lazarus was released after Jesus gave thanks to the Father.

Thanksgiving releases the power of God into difficult and even seemingly impossible situations. Learn to give thanks to the Father always, even when great needs and challenges are staring you in the face. At Lazarus' tomb, Jesus gave thanks to the Father for answered prayers. He also thanked the Father for answers to His previous requests. In fact, He went on to thank the Father for hearing Him always and, for that matter, His continuous stream of answered prayer.

Have you thanked God for His answers to your prayers in the past? When you face a challenging situation, remember that He is a prayer-answering God. Thank Him for the answered prayers in your life and call forth the miracles you need. When you do, God's power will be released into the challenging situations in your life, and you will see miraculous answers to your prayers.

CHAPTER ELEVEN

DEVELOPING THE HABIT OF THANKFULNESS

EXPRESSING GRATITUDE TO anyone who blesses us is a cherished value in many cultures across the world. It is an important part of the good values many parents instill in their children. However, today's fast-paced world leaves us with little time to ponder our blessings and return, like the one grateful leper did, to adequately express gratitude to our benefactors. Sadly, the cultural value of thanksgiving is being abandoned in many societies today.

Worse than this is when a failure to give thanks extends to our relationship with God; then we risk becoming like either the children of Israel during their wilderness journey or the nine lepers who forgot about the Lord Jesus Christ in their hurry to obtain their certification. In the absence of a deliberate pursuit of a life of thanksgiving to God and to those whom He uses to bless us, we may be filled with the poison of complaining, murmuring and grumbling at our perceived lack and never know the joy of contentment or how to bring satisfaction to God our Father through our gratitude and thanksgiving.

To help us cultivate an inner propensity to be grateful and express gratitude like the leper, we ought to carefully consider the exercise below. Using the thirty-one Scripture verses provided about thanksgiving, find one reason each day to thank God.

Psychologists claim that it takes twenty-one days of consistently performing a positive action to break its opposing negative habit. If you have been caught up in the same web of ingratitude as the children of Israel and find yourself habitually failing to give thanks to God for His goodness and mercy in the face of difficulties, an intentional expression of gratitude on a daily basis for the next thirty-one days may be of help to you.

These thirty-one verses admonish us to express our gratitude to God for who He is, what He has done and all that He continues to do for us—His children. We should then make time in each day, preferably when we first wake up, to express our thanksgiving to God for those reasons, regardless of what we might be going through at the time. Furthermore, we should firmly resolve not to complain, murmur or grumble. Hebrews 13:16 admonishes us to ensure that the fruit of our lips is thanksgiving to God.

The verses for the first fifteen days are from the book of Psalms, and some of the reasons given there may seem repetitive, but that is good for our exercise. Instead of feeling it is repetitive, we should realize that since God does not change but remains the same, we can thank Him over and over again, even on daily basis, for the same attributes that we see in Him daily. Doing so will enable us to break the evil habit of ingratitude to God and acquire a new habit of thankfulness.

During this exercise, we need to keep in mind that, more than breaking an evil pattern, our goal is to cultivate a heart of appreciation for what we have been given from the good hand of our God. Without appreciation in the heart first of all, any attempt to impose an external rule will be in vain. It is my prayer first that each participant will have the eyes of your understanding enlightened that you may know that our God is good and deserves to be thanked every day. Hebrews 13:15 appropriately exhorts us in this manner: *"Therefore by Him let us continually offer the sacrifice of praise to God, that is, the fruit of our lips, giving thanks to His name."* Even when it is a sacrifice, we must commit ourselves to giving thanks with a grateful heart.

Let me encourage you to spend the next 31 days reading the designated passage, meditating on the verse, then give thanks to God for the attribute mentioned in the passage.

> "Gratitude makes sense of our past, brings peace for for today, creates a vision for tomorrow."
> —Melody Beattie

31 Days of Gratitude

Day 1:

Psalm 30:4 – *Sing praise to the Lord, you saints of His, and give thanks at the remembrance of His holy name.*

Thank God for His Attributes: God is holy.

DAY 2:

Psalm 50:13-15 – *Will I eat the flesh of bulls, or drink the blood of goats? Offer to God thanksgiving, and pay your vows to the Most High. Call upon Me in the day of trouble; I will deliver you, and you shall glorify Me.*

Thank God for His Attributes: God is our deliverer.

DAY 3:

Psalm 69:29-31a – *But I am poor and sorrowful; Let Your salvation, O God, set me up on high. I will praise the name of God with a song, and will magnify Him with thanksgiving. This also shall please the* LORD *better than an ox or bull. .*

Thank God for His Attributes: God's salvation sets me up on high. He is my Lifter and my Savior.

DAY 4:

Psalm 75:1 – *We give thanks to You, O God, we give thanks! For Your wondrous works declare that Your name is near.*

Thank God for His Attributes: God performs wondrous works and shows through them that He is near.

DAY 5:

Psalm 92:1-2 – *It is good to give thanks to the* LORD, *and to sing praises to Your name, O Most High; to declare Your lovingkindness in the morning, and Your faithfulness every night.*

Thank God for His Attributes: God shows His lovingkindness and faithfulness to us.

DAY 6:

Psalm 95:1-3 – *Oh come, let us sing to the Lord! Let us shout joyfully to the Rock of our salvation. Let us come before His presence with thanksgiving; Let us shout joyfully to Him with psalms. For the Lord is the great God, and the great king above all gods.*

Thank God for His Attributes: God is the Rock of our salvation and greater than all other gods.

DAY 7:

Psalm 100:3-4 – *Know that the Lord, He is God; it is He who has made us, and not we ourselves; we are His people and the sheep of His pasture. Enter into His gates with thanksgiving, and into His courts with praise. Be thankful to Him, and bless His name.*

Thank God for His Attributes: God is our Maker and our Shepherd.

DAY 8:

Psalm 105:1-2 – *Oh, give thanks to the Lord! Call upon His name; make known His deeds among the peoples! Sing to Him, sing psalms to Him; Talk of all His wondrous works!*

Thank God for His Attributes: His deeds are mighty among His people; His works are wondrous to behold.

DAY 9:

Psalm 106:1 – *Praise the LORD! Oh, give thanks to the LORD, for He is good! For His mercy endures forever.*

Thank God for His Attributes: God is good.

DAY 10:

Psalm 107:1 – *Oh, give thanks to the LORD, for He is good! For His mercy endures forever.*

Thank God for His Attributes: God's mercy endures forever.

DAY 11:

Psalm 107:8-9 – *Oh, that men would give thanks to the Lord for His goodness, and for His wonderful works to the children of men! For He satisfies the longing soul, and fills the hungry soul with goodness.*

Thank God for His Attributes: God satisfies our souls with His goodness.

DAY 12:

Psalm 116:16-17 – *O LORD, truly I am Your servant; I am Your servant, the son of Your maidservant; You have loosed my bonds. I will offer to You the sacrifice of thanksgiving, and will call upon the name of the LORD.*

Thank God for His Attributes: God is our bondage breaker! He loosed my bonds.

Day 13:

Psalm 118:1 – *Oh, give thanks to the Lord, for He is good! For His mercy endures forever.*

Thank God for His Attributes: God is merciful and good.

Day 14:

Psalm 136:1-2 – *Oh, give thanks to the Lord, for He is good! For His mercy endures forever. Oh, give thanks to the God of gods! For His mercy endures forever. Oh, give thanks to the Lord of Lords! For His mercy endures forever.*

Thank God for His Attributes: God is merciful and good.

Day 15:

Psalm 136:26 – *Oh, give thanks to the God of heaven! For His mercy endures forever.*

Thank God for His Attributes: God's mercy endures forever.

Day 16:

I Chronicles 16:8 – *Oh, give thanks to the Lord! Call upon His name; make known His deeds among the peoples.*

Thank God for His Attributes: God's deeds show that He works on our behalf.

DAY 17:

I Chronicles 16:34 – *Oh, give thanks to the LORD, for He is good; For His mercy endures forever.*

Thank God for His Attributes: God is good and merciful.

DAY 18:

I Chronicles 29:12-13 – *Both riches and honor come from You, and You reign over all. In Your hand is power and might; In Your hand it is to make great and to give strength to all. Now therefore, our God, we thank You and praise Your glorious name.*

Thank God for His Attributes: God is the Giver of riches and honor. He is the Source of greatness; He makes one great. He is the Giver of strength.

DAY 19:

Jeremiah 30:19 – *Then out of them shall proceed thanksgiving and the voice of those who make merry. I will multiply them, and they shall not diminish; I will also glorify them, and they shall not be small.*

Thank God for His Attributes: God multiplies His people; He is the Source of our increase.

DAY 20:

Colossians 3:17 – *And whatever you do in word or deed, do all in the name of the Lord Jesus, giving thanks to God the Father through Him.*

Thank God for His Attributes: God is our Father.

Day 21:

1 Corinthians 1:4-5 – *I thank my God always concerning you for the grace of God which was given to you by Christ Jesus, that you were enriched in everything by Him in all utterance and all knowledge.*

Thank God for His Attributes: God gives us His grace.

Day 22:

1 Corinthians 15:57 – *But thanks be to God, who gives us the victory through our Lord Jesus Christ.*

Thank God for His Attributes: God gives us victory over death and Hell through His Son.

Day 23:

2 Corinthians 2:14 – *Now thanks be to God who always leads us in triumph in Christ, and through us diffuses the fragrance of His knowledge in every place.*

Thank God for His Attributes: God leads us in triumph and not in defeat.

Day 24:

2 Corinthians 4:15 – *For all things are for your sakes, that the abundant grace might through the thanksgiving of many redound to the glory of God.*

Thank God for His Attributes: God shows us abundant grace.

DAY 25:

2 Corinthians 9:15 – *Thanks be to God for His indescribable gift!*

Thank God for His Attributes: God gave His Son to save us.

DAY 26:

Ephesians 1:15-16 – *Therefore I also, after I heard of your faith in the Lord Jesus and your love for all the saints, do not cease to give thanks for you, making mention of you in my prayers.*

Thank God for His Attributes: God is the Source of our faith in His Son and the Source of our love for the saints.

DAY 27:

I Timothy 4:4-5 – *For every creature of God is good, and nothing is to be refused if it is received with thanksgiving; for it is sanctified by the word of God and prayer.*

Thank God for His Attributes: God is the Creator and Giver of all good things.

DAY 28:

Colossians 3:15 – *And let the peace of God rule in your hearts, to which also you were called in one body; and be thankful.*

Thank God for His Attributes: God gives us peace.

DAY 29:

Colossians 3:17 – *And whatever you do in word or deed, do all in* *the name of the Lord Jesus, giving thanks to God the Father through Him.*

Thank God for His Attributes: God is our Father.

Day 30:

Colossians 4:2-3 – *Continue earnestly in prayer, being vigilant in it with thanksgiving; meanwhile praying also for us, that God would open to us a door for the word, to speak the mystery of Christ, for which I am also in chains.*

Thank God for His Attributes: God opens doors (opportunities) for His children. And when He opens doors, they remain open—no one can shut them.

Day 31:

Philippians 4:6-7 – *Be anxious for nothing, but in everything by prayer and supplication, with thanksgiving, let your requests be made known to God; and the peace of God, which passes all under-standing, will guard your hearts and minds through Christ Jesus.*

Thank God for His Attributes: God gives peace to us; His peace guards our hearts and minds always.

~

The best way to show your gratitude to God is to receive the Lord Jesus Christ in your heart as your personal Savior and the Lord of your life. Sin is like a spiritual leprosy that has wounded, disfigured and ravaged lives. You can be healed of the leprosy of sin in your life by believing on the Lord Jesus Christ as your Savior, accepting the sacrifice He made on the cross as the price that He paid for your salvation, and inviting Him to come into your heart. If you do not have the assurance that you will spend eternity in Heaven, God's Word clearly tells us how to accept Christ as our Savior so that we can be saved from an eternity in Hell. Please allow me to share several verses with you that will explain how you can have the assurance of Heaven when your life here on this earth is over.

SALVATION CORNER

1) **First of all, we must recognize that we are all sinners.** *"For all have sinned, and come short of the glory of God"* (Romans 3:23).

Sin is the wrong we do—lying, stealing, murdering, etc. According to Romans 3:10, no one is innocent: *"As it is written, There is none righteous, no, not one."*

2) **God says there is a penalty or consequence for our sin.** *"For the wages of sin is death…"* (Romans 6:23a).

Wages is like a payment. Just like we receive wages or payment for work we do at a job, or just like a criminal has to pay the penalty for his crime, God says there is a payment (wages) due to us for our sin… and that payment or penalty is death.

This word *death* refers not only to a physical death—when our body dies and is put in the grave. It refers also to a spiritual death, meaning that our eternal soul is forever separated from God in a place the Bible describes as a lake of fire, a place of fire and brimstone and eternal punishment. *"And death and hell were cast into the lake of fire. This is the second death. And whosoever was not found written in the book of life was cast into the lake of fire"* (Revelation 20:14-15).

See also Revelation 19:20 and 20:10.

3) Romans 5:12 tells us where sin came from. *"Wherefore as by one man* [Adam] *sin entered into the world, and death by sin, and so death passed upon all men, for that all have sinned."*

When Adam chose to sin in the Garden of Eden, all men since then have been born under the penalty of sin. You might be thinking, How is that fair? I wasn't in the Garden of Eden. I didn't make that choice; Adam did.

4) God is always just and did not leave us alone to pay that penalty of death for our sins. *"But God commendeth His love toward us, in that, while we were yet sinners, Christ died for us"* (Romans 5:8).

God is always a just God. Therefore, He determined that if one man (Adam) could make all men sinners, then one Man (Jesus), could pay sin's penalty for all mankind. *"For as by one man's disobedience many were made sinners, so by the obedience of one shall many be made righteous"* (Romans 5:19). God showed His love toward us by giving His only son, Jesus Christ, to die in our place. Jesus' death paid the penalty for our sins. Not just anyone could pay this penalty for us, but because Jesus was a perfect sacrifice, He alone was qualified to pay for our sins. He died on the cross, was buried in a tomb, and three days later rose from the dead—victorious over death and Hell—so that we might have eternal life in Heaven.

5) **In Romans 6:23 above, we saw the penalty for our sin, but the rest of that verse tells us what God gave us through His Son's death on the cross.** *"For the wages of sin is death; but the gift of God is eternal life through Jesus Christ our Lord."*

God's gift to us is eternal life in Heaven—paid for by the death of His Son, Jesus. Think with me for a moment about the word *gift*. Let's say that I purchased a very valuable gift for you and left it on your porch. Then I called you and told you it was there.

You can **know** about that gift and understand that it is a valuable gift. You can **believe** the gift is waiting for you to open it. But if you leave that gift on your porch and never open it and claim it as your own, it won't do you any good no matter its value.

God's gift of salvation is the same way.

We can **know** about God's gift of eternal life. We can even **believe** that Jesus died to pay for our sins and that He wants to save us…but if we never accept that gift for our very own, it does us no good at all.

Unless we accept God's gift, we will still die in our sins and go to Hell forever. So, the question is, how do we accept that gift?

6) **Romans 10:9-13 tells us how to accept God's gift of eternal life.** *That if thou shalt confess with thy mouth the Lord Jesus, and shalt believe in thine heart that God hath raised him from the dead, thou shalt be saved. [10]For with the heart man believeth unto righteousness; and*

with the mouth confession is made unto salvation. [11]For the scripture saith, Whosoever believeth on him shall not be ashamed. [12]For there is no difference between the Jew and the Greek: for the same Lord over all is rich unto all that call upon him. [13]For whosoever shall call upon the name of the Lord shall be saved.

Today, God is offering you the free gift of salvation—He is willing to forgive you of your sins and give you the gift of eternal life. All you need to do is ask. Verse 13 uses the word whosoever. That means anyone…that means you.

Ephesians 2:8-9 tells us, *"For by grace are ye saved through faith; and that not of yourselves: it is the gift of God. Not of works, lest any man should boast."* *Grace* means "unmerited favor"—you can't earn salvation. This verse is clear that salvation is not obtained by our works. We cannot do good deeds, give money to the church, or do anything else in exchange for salvation. Only God's free gift can save us from Hell. God has already done everything required for us to have the gift of eternal life when He gave His Son to die in our place.

If you realize that you are a sinner on your way to Hell, you can accept God's gift today by calling on the Lord and asking Him to save you. If you would like to do that, but feel you don't know what to say, you can pray the prayer below—keeping in mind that it's not any specific set of words that saves you. You are saved by believing on Jesus and trusting Him as your only way to Heaven. If you want to ask Jesus to save you, pray this prayer:

"God, I know I'm a sinner who deserves Hell. But I believe Jesus

Christ paid for my sins when He died on the cross and rose again from the dead. Please forgive me of my sin and take me to Heaven when I die. I put my trust in Jesus Christ and what He did on the cross as my only way to Heaven. Thank You giving me the gift of eternal life. Amen."

If you prayed that prayer, according to what the Bible says, you will spend eternity with God in Heaven. God's Word promises that, because of Jesus' death on our behalf, we will never be condemned for our sins. *"There is therefore now no condemnation to them which are in Christ Jesus, who walk not after the flesh, but after the Spirit"* (Romans 8:1). The Bible also says we can have a relationship of peace with God through Jesus Christ. *"Therefore being justified by faith, we have peace with God through our Lord Jesus Christ"* (Romans 5:21). Finally, we have this promise from God: *"For I am persuaded, that neither death, nor life, nor angels, nor principalities, nor powers, nor things present, nor things to come, Nor height, nor depth, nor any other creature, shall be able to separate us from the love of God, which is in Christ Jesus our Lord"* (Romans 8:38-39).

If you have placed your trust in Christ for salvation as a result of reading this book, it would be a great blessing to me if you would please let me know by emailing me at pastorwisdom@gracechapelint.org.